D1311013

THE DEATH OF SLAVERY

The Death

THE CHICAGO HISTORY OF AMERICAN CIVILIZATION

Daniel J. Boorstin, EDITOR

# of Slavery

The United States, 1837–65

Elbert B. Smith

THE UNIVERSITY OF CHICAGO PRESS

CHICAGO AND LONDON

ISBN: 0–226–76395–1 (clothbound); 0–226–76397–8 (paperbound)
Library of Congress Catalog Card Number: 67–16779

THE UNIVERSITY OF CHICAGO PRESS, CHICAGO 60637
The University of Chicago Press, Ltd., London

89 88 87 86 85 84 83   6 7 8 9
Printed in the United States of America

to
Jean
with love

Editor's Preface

The coming of the Civil War has been distorted by two kinds of hindsight. First, there has been the argument that the war was "inevitable." Nothing is more difficult than imagining that things could have been otherwise. Second, there has been the argument that the war was a simple conflict between Good and Evil. The Americans fighting for the Union, we are told, were consciously engaged in a holy crusade, while those on the other side were conscious champions of slavery. To ask ourselves simply, "Why was the war inevitable?" or "Why were so many Americans against freedom?" is to miss the actual experience of most of the people of those years. To sense what it was really like to be alive then, we must try to see the choices those men saw.

Elbert B. Smith, in this history of the United States from 1837 to 1865, puts his spotlight on the actual choices that men faced. He is more interested in what they saw ahead of them

Editor's Preface

than in what we can see behind us. Mr. Smith has the great advantage over most historians of the era, that he has personally immersed himself in the democratic process. Having run for elective office, he has seen what kinds of issues do, and do not, reach the people. By his grasp of the intriguing intricacies of political history, he helps us understand how personal strengths and weaknesses made certain issues seem crucial, and certain compromises impossible. The Civil War, according to Mr. Smith, cannot be adequately summarized as the product either of inevitability or of morality.

In the later twentieth century we should not need to be reminded that the Civil War left many questions unsettled. The travail of our own time—our continuing struggle to realize the ideals of our Founders—should remind us that to oversimplify any era in history is to befog the tasks of later generations.

The "Chicago History of American Civilization" aims to bring to the general reader, in compact and readable form, the insights of scholars who write from different points of view. This series contains two kinds of books: a *chronological* group, which will provide a coherent narrative of American history from its beginning to the present day, and a *topical* group which will deal with the history of varied and significant aspects of American life. This is a volume in the chronological group. Those which have already been published are listed at the end of this volume.

DANIEL J. BOORSTIN

Table of Contents

I

Historians Have Said...

During the period 1837–65, the United States endured depressions, enjoyed immense progress and prosperity, and acquired a vast western empire in a foreign war. The democratic ideology enunciated by Jefferson and brought to a climax by the time of Andrew Jackson continued to gain strength and become a vital part of the American scene. Political parties won and lost elections, national policies often succeeded and sometimes failed, many conflicts were settled by debate and compromise, and many remained unsettled. Meanwhile, the population grew and prospered on its patrimony of magnificent natural resources and almost unlimited space.

In 1861, however, this idyllic scene was shattered by the guns of Fort Sumter, and more than 600,000 men died before peace was restored. This overshadowing event by necessity becomes the central theme of any history of this period.

The Death of Slavery

Any study dealing with the coming of the American Civil War is certain to provide more unanswerable questions than unquestionable answers. Why did the democratic system of debate, compromise, and acceptance of compromise—a system whereby Americans were supposed to settle their quarrels, competitions, and conflicts with words instead of weapons—break down in 1861? Why did men who shared a common heritage, common language, and common loyalties finally resort to that most undemocratic of all expedients, war? Was the war inevitable? Was it necessary? Do those who argue that perhaps the war was unnecessary deserve the usual accusation that they are insufficiently alert to the moral evil of slavery? Could the wicked institution of slavery have been destroyed without the carnage of war? Did the differences in geography, climate, economic development, and social institutions make necessary the deaths of more than 600,000 Americans and the suffering of millions of others?

Is the study of this period in American life a mere survey of great sweeping impersonal deterministic forces which shaped human destinies regardless of what men as individuals could have done? Certainly the long growing season and warmer weather affected the development of the South. The cold winters, rocky soil, rugged coastline, and rich industrial power from swiftly flowing rivers shaped the character of New England. The economic versatility and the cosmopolitan character of the population of the middle Atlantic states and certain border states made them strongholds of the spirit of compromise. The wealth of resources to the west, coupled with magnificent natural systems of water transportation, helped make an interdependent nation and create a northwestern region ready to fight for the preservation of a national union. The very existence of slavery in an exuberant new land dedicated to freedom and equality of opportunity, and racing toward the technological miracles of the twentieth century, was an anachronism which could have no future. And hovering over all was a religious tradition which divided the world into good and evil and forbade compromise on questions involving moral righteousness and wickedness.

Modern man, however, is compelled to seek a faith in the existence of a wide variety and range of independent human behavior within the limits of such determinisms. The belief that man is a free moral agent who will succeed or fail, prosper or suffer, and survive or be destroyed on the basis of his own actions, is necessary for responsible human behavior at any level. This belief is also man's best antidote to intolerant ideologies whose followers claim to be in step with the world's predetermined future and thereby derive special authority to inflict cruelties against their fellowmen. The deterministic view of history all too often produces either the pessimist who sees no value in constructive effort or the fanatic eager to shape the world to his own pattern regardless of the cost.

If, therefore, the years leading to America's great tragedy are to shed useful light on the dilemmas of the modern world, the situations, decisions, actions, and events of the period must be viewed as manmade or at least man-affected phenomena which might have been different and which need not be repeated. Some historians have called this period the first cold war. Those who would help keep the present cold war from ending like the first can learn much from a careful study of this earlier American experience.

Immediately following the American Civil War, each section, naturally enough, wrote its own story of why it all happened. In the North the war became a great crusade fought to free human beings from bondage. In the history texts Northern heroes led by the martyr Abraham Lincoln joined a noble struggle against the immoral, undemocratic, and unchristian evil of slavery and marched away to die to make men free. The war ended slavery; the war, therefore, was fought for that purpose.

This soul-satisfying, heart-warming, inspiring, but grossly oversimplified view still has its warm defenders. In the modern version, the South never would have abandoned slavery without war; slavery was a moral evil too wicked for toleration by civilized men; those, therefore, who question the inevitability of the war and suggest the possibility of an eventually peaceful settlement are sentimental appeasers unwilling to come to grips with harsh realities.

This interpretation, however, is badly weakened by the admitted fact that most Northern leaders in 1861, including Lincoln, emphatically denied any inclination to injure Southern slavery. The Republican presidential convention of 1860 passed over the party's longtime leader, William H. Seward, because of his connections with radical abolitionism, and the party's platform contained pledges that Southern slavery would remain undisturbed. Lincoln's speeches, including his first inaugural address, repeated this theme over and over. Indeed, Lincoln also pledged himself as President to enforce the federal laws designed to help Southerners recover fugitive slaves. When General Frémont, in the early part of the war, freed the slaves in Missouri by proclamation, Lincoln promptly revoked the action and discharged Frémont lest Missouri be driven to secession. "My paramount object in this struggle," Lincoln wrote Horace Greeley in 1862, "is to save the Union and *is not* either to save or destroy slavery. If I could save the Union without freeing

4

any slaves, I would do it; if I could save it by freeing *all* the slaves, I would do it; and if I could do it by freeing some and leaving others alone, I would also do that."

Abraham Lincoln spoke for a northwestern region which practiced various proscriptions against free Negroes and which objected to slavery primarily for economic reasons. He also spoke for men everywhere who were dedicated to the preservation of the national state created by the founding fathers. Such men were driven by the powerful spirit of nationalism which swept through the nineteenth century world to create national states in Germany and Italy and leave a powerful desire for national independence among subject peoples everywhere.

Nationalism had a further dimension in the United States. To Lincoln and many other Americans the United States was a great experiment in freedom and self-government which for the sake of the entire human race must not be allowed to fail. Those honored at Gettysburg, said Lincoln in his immortal address, had died that "government of the people, by the people, for the people, shall not perish from the earth."

Southern secession threatened to destroy this experiment by proving the incompatibility of democracy and national unity, and slavery thereby became a symbol of disunion which must be destroyed for the salvation of America itself. Then and then only did abolition become a practical threat to Southern slavery.

Southern radicals, however, refused to believe Lincoln's assurances. They made the right to expand slavery into new territories a test of future Northern intentions, and when Lincoln and his party refused to yield on this question they struck for an independent South.

That the fire-eaters reached such a decision is less remarkable than their ability to get the Southern people to follow it, since only a fourth of them had any direct relation with slavery. In the end the Southern excuse for secession was a denial of the right to take slavery into territories where the institution would have been virtually impossible because of geography, climate, or the attitudes of the people already there.

The most popular Southern version has rested largely upon the constitutional defense of Alexander H. Stephens and Jefferson Davis. According to this view the Constitution guaranteed slavery, the North refused to abide by these constitutional principles, and the South, therefore, was compelled to leave the Union for its own protection. John C. Calhoun and the Southern extremists, runs this interpretation, were really great nationalists who strove to preserve the Union of the founding fathers and left it only when the North had converted it into an instrument of tyranny against the Southern way of life.

This interpretation, like the popular Northern view, is much too simple. To be sure, the Constitution recognized slavery by awarding the South white representatives in Congress for three-fifths of the slave population. It protected slavery as property under the due process of law clause, and the Supreme Court unanimously affirmed the constitutionality of federal laws designed to help recapture fugitive slaves. The timeless idealism of the Declaration of Independence, which says that *all* men are created free and equal, was not copied into the infinitely more conservative Constitution. The freedom-granting Thirteenth, Fourteenth, and Fifteenth Amendments did not come until after the Civil War. The abolitionist, William Lloyd Garrison, once burned the Constitution publicly and pronounced it "a covenant with death and an agreement with hell." William H. Seward became famous for his talk about the "higher law" of

God which placed human freedom above all legal documents and manmade laws, and therefore outranked the Constitution on the subject of slavery.

When Southerners, however, sought to extend their constitutional doctrines to the question of taking slavery to new territories, they were on weak ground. Indeed, the South finally worked itself into a constitutional dilemma. Its leaders presented a states' rights argument for a federal government too weak to keep slavery out of new territories, and in the next breath demanded a federal government with power to impose slavery on new territories regardless of the wishes of the inhabitants. In the 1840's, John C. Calhoun spun his involved doctrines against the right of the federal government to prohibit territorial slavery. Yet the Northwest Ordinance of 1787, which barred slavery in the area north of the Ohio River, and the Missouri Compromise of 1820, which barred slavery in the vast area north of the southern border of Missouri between the Mississippi River and the Rockies, had been written and overwhelmingly supported by Southerners. By 1848 many Southern leaders were strongly opposing the right of the federal government to prohibit slavery in the territories. In 1857 this "new" Southern position was upheld by the Supreme Court in the Dred Scott case, but the many decades of Southern acceptance and support of the earlier principle invalidated it as a justification for war.

The Southern social system and way of life were indeed being threatened, but not by Northern abolitionists. Americans were on their way to a new world of scientific and technological miracles—an industrial world with which an agrarian way of life built upon slavery could not compete and an ideological world in which human slavery would be intolerable.

7

The Death of Slavery

Threats and fears are more endurable, however, when they can be identified in terms of enemies who can be seen, understood, and fought against directly. Northern opponents of slavery provided Southerners with simple, emotionally satisfying, but dangerous answers to the difficult problems that would eventually have to be faced. The suffering and destruction of the Civil War would neither solve the problems nor make them easier.

As time passed, historians who continued to see the war as a crusade against slavery found forgiveness for the South in the forces of climate, geography, and soils which had enabled the institution to thrive. In this view slavery was a burden rather than a sin, and the Southerners were victims of circumstances. James Ford Rhodes blamed the technology of cotton-raising. Woodrow Wilson found the war to be a product of growth and evolution. Southerners like William E. Dodd and Ulrich B. Phillips defended their section as one of many virtues which had done its best with its faults and problems. Other Southerners like Frank Owsley and Charles Ramsdell continued to reject the olive branch.

The deterministic philosophy so prevalent at the turn of the nineteenth century ultimately produced the view of Charles Beard and various followers that slavery did not cause the war at all. These writers saw the Civil War as the final stage in the ancient quarrel between Hamilton and Jefferson over whether America would become a land of commerce and industry or remain dominated by agriculture. In this view the North wanted a powerful, unified, paternalistic central government which could provide high tariffs, sound national banking, the removal of immigration barriers and easy importation of foreign labor, subsidies to railroad builders, uniform protection for business in all the states, and sundry other services. Because the agrarian South had successfully opposed all these things in the name of states' rights but had begun to feel its power slipping, and because the North was determined to have these policies, the two sections eventually went to war to settle the question. This interpretation is important. Certainly economic competition contributed much to the animosities which brought on the war. This version, however, reads result into causation and as a single explanation is grossly inadequate. It exaggerates the economic uniformity within each section, ignores the Northwest as a separate section, and incorrectly minimizes the great moral question of slavery and the emotional drive of nationalism. Indeed, the United States in the 1850's had already demonstrated a remarkable capacity for producing industrial wealth without significant government assistance.

Economic differences were compromised when moral issues were not involved, but the question of extending slavery created a point beyond which compromises could not go. Sacrificing personal integrity by compromising moral right and wrong is difficult for honest men anywhere, and nineteenth-century Americans were thoroughly steeped in the tradition of religious salvation through righteousness and eternal damnation through wickedness. To argue that Americans might have had a civil war without the slavery quarrel is nonsense. Moreover, the men who flocked to the colors to put down Southern armed rebellion and save the Union did not see themselves as part of an economic contest, and neither did Abraham Lincoln.

A related interpretation has blamed the war on deep-seated social, economic, and psychological differences. Certainly the industrial Northeast differed from the agrarian South, and the

The Death of Slavery

Northwest differed from both, but Americans in 1861 were far more alike than different. A majority in every state, including those of the South, were small, independent farmers. Americans spoke the same language, joined the same nationwide church organizations, voted for and against the same political parties, loved the same flag, sang the same "Star-Spangled Banner," and loved the same Union. They shared a common history, economic interdependence, and kinfolk in every section. Cultural differences alone in a nation already noted for its melting pot characteristics would not have produced a civil war.

The horrors of World War I and its disillusioning aftermath, the threats to democracy inherent in the fanaticisms of Fascism and Communism, the world's journey to the brink of destruction in World War II, and the continuing threat of the cold war, created an atmosphere for the development of a new approach to the Civil War. Beginning in the late 1930's, historians like Avery Craven, James Randall, and Allan Nevins began questioning the inevitability of the war and stressing the mistakes, failures, and hypocrisies of the political leaders and opinion-makers in both sections. In this "revisionist" view the war became a breakdown in the democratic system of government brought about in part by growing economic, social, and value differences, and in part by the creation of false images of each section in the eyes of the other; events and situations were distorted and exaggerated by partisan politicians, the press, writers, and the churches, until ordinary people and generations of later historians completely lost sight of the actual facts.

The revisionist historians exploded many earlier myths and produced historical narratives infinitely more accurate in detail. They also made a powerful case for moderation, gradual and non-violent progress, avoidance of fanaticism, responsibility in partisan politics, and the long view of history.

Their chances for a universal following, however, foundered on the insoluble question of slavery. Various Southern critics remained unwilling to admit that men had died to defend an institution not necessarily in danger. Northerners were reluctant to surrender their glow of moral superiority to a view which reduced the sentiments of the "Battle Hymn of the Republic" to an afterthought. The revisionists were charged with blindness to the moral evil of slavery and were compelled by the logic of their position to argue that slavery might have been tolerated for a few more years and that the institution might have died peacefully if the war had been avoided. Abraham Lincoln had once taken exactly the same position. The first argument, however, was subject to easy distortion, and the second was unprovable. Among the critics, Kenneth Stampp and others dwelt on the profitability of slavery and argued that it might have gone on forever without the war, while Arthur Schlesinger, Jr., drew upon the world's sad experience with appeasement of the Nazis during the 1930's to conclude that in 1861 violence was the only realistic solution to an inescapable moral dilemma.

Few, however, could quarrel with the basic revisionist theme that men should strive for peaceful solutions even to their most difficult problems and irreconcilable conflicts and that such solutions become more difficult when truth, realism, and rational calculations of interest succumb to emotionalism, pride, and fears based upon partisan distortions and exaggerations. Even fewer could fail to hope that these lessons of the nineteenth century would not be wasted upon the twentieth.

II

There Were Sections

The New England corner of the United States is a region of granite and ice. In past ages the glaciers covered the land with rocks and a thin topsoil which would offer little to future farmers. Certain compensating resources remained, however. Swift rivers would turn factory wheels and later produce electricity. A rugged coastline with deep bays and many islands provided great harbors for oceangoing trade. Magnificent forests of conifers and hardwoods provided the timbers for the greatest sailing vessels ever built by man. Great underwater banks furnished a rich harvest of fish. Colonial New Englanders soon developed into woodworkers, furniture-makers, shipbuilders, sailors, fishermen, and tradesmen.

For the early settlers New England was a rough, stingy, cold environment, but the English Calvinist Puritans were more than

There Were Sections

a match for it. They had left sinful England to prove that in a new world men could build a holy commonwealth ruled by the laws of God. They considered their problems and misfortunes to be God's testing devices, and hard work and endurance of adversity provided opportunities for proving their election to the kingdom of heaven. The holy commonwealth required constant attention to the ills and evils of society, as well as to the morals of its citizens, and it was no coincidence that most of the great mid-nineteenth-century reform movements in America originated in New England. New Englanders stressed self-examination, schools, churches, and social responsibility. Calvinist theology taught that man was naturally depraved, and that though creating wealth was godly, enjoying it was sinful. Wealth, after all, was a gift from God, and its possessor was to administer it as a steward administers the property of his employer. Indeed, almost any pleasure, because of its temptations to excess, was dangerous. Even the doctrine that unbaptized infants were condemned to hellfire was still preached in the early nineteenth century. The New England God was a god of anger, unbending justice, and adequate punishment, who divided men into the righteous and unrighteous and had little time for the in-between.

The industrial boom triggered by the War of 1812 brought new ways of living to New England. The earlier small factories gave way to major industries, and the region soon found itself with the problems as well as the advantages of urban industrialism.

The first labor supply came from the farms. New England industrialization coincided with a great population thrust into western New York and the Great Lakes region, and this opening of new soils gave New England agriculture severe competition. Many rural young people either joined the trek westward or moved into the industrial towns and cities.

Soon long black wagons, the original Black Marias, were going up and down the villages picking up young girls for work in the new textile mills. Recruiting advertisements promised parents their daughters would live in closely supervised dormitories, be marched regularly to church, and be carefully regulated as to moral habits. The image of factory work as a highly moral and religious experience aided substantially in the recruitment of thousands of new laborers, poetically described by Whittier as the "fair, unveiled nuns of industry."

Young men also worked in the factories, as well as a great many wives and children. Factories would hire entire families by contracting with the father for the services of his household. In 1820, 45 per cent of the workers in New England factories were children under twelve. Wages and working conditions varied from place to place, and in some areas there was genuine enlightenment, but generally the hours were long and the pay was low.

In the beginning, however, there was considerable harmony among employers and employees. The young laborers were often fugitives from cold, harsh, and lonely farms, and the opportunity to work twelve to fourteen hours a day in the company of other young people seemed an improvement over their previous life. Also, the early industrial leaders were often men who knew their workers personally and were endowed with a considerable sense of social responsibility.

Time, however, soon produced a new generation of workers who had no memories of an older way of life and who wanted more and better things for themselves. Simultaneously, British competition was driving down the price of cotton cloth all over the world, and employers were finding themselves less rather than more willing to grant either higher wages or better working conditions. Also, the factory builders and their heirs were in many cases moving from the factory towns to the more luxurious coastal cities like Boston and Newport and were leaving their industries in the hands of managers responsible only for profits. All this helped bring to New England many of the worst features of industrialism in its early stages: periodic depressions and unemployment, relatively low wages and poor working conditions, poverty, insecurity for the sick and the aged, slums, juvenile delinquency, crime, and labor conflicts.

Employers frequently found it easier to change workers than to change conditions. Wagons began to bring in French Canadian girls to spin the cloth, and ships began to unload young Irish men and women by the hundreds. The fierce competition for jobs was compounded by the fact that most of the newcomers were Roman Catholics, and ancient religious conflicts were soon revived in all their bitterness.

The New England transition to a new way of life was painful, but among people reared in the Calvinist tradition it provided the impetus for the greatest age of reform in American history. Throughout New England and indeed throughout the entire Northeast, new attitudes swept through the churches and intellectual circles. Religious leaders in great revival movements as well as in the older churches began stressing the gospel of Christ in terms of the duty of men to help and serve each other. Some like William Ellery Channing formed the new Unitarian Church, which almost entirely ignored the supernatural and put its faith in religion as a way of life on earth rather than as a ticket to heaven. Others became agnostics in the pattern of the labor reformers Robert Dale Owen and

The Death of Slavery

Frances Wright. Ralph Waldo Emerson led the transcendentalists, who believed that the essential nobility of man's nature transcended his experience and environment. Emerson felt that man was in every way created in the image of God and that there was no height unattainable by man. Indeed, most of the reformers of the period shared this new faith in the essential perfectibility of man as well as the duty of every man to work for a more perfect world.

Freedom's ferment occasionally took unusual shapes. Joseph Smith of Vermont discovered the golden books of Mormon and founded a religious sect noted for the collective economic responsibility assumed by its members. The practice of polygamy brought persecution which pushed the saints across the continent until they founded their own state of Utah. For others seeking escape there was William Miller, whose biblical scholarship led him to the conclusion that Christ would return in 1843 to gather up the faithful, raise the dead, and reward the saints. Aided somewhat by the tail of a comet which throughout 1843 hung across the noonday sky like a poised sword, Miller won more than a million converts. On the appointed day many of the Millerites gave away property, tearfully bade loved ones good-bye, donned their white ascension robes, and waited for a judgment that did not come. The effort to avoid an evil world and return to true principles led also to various communal experiments like Brook Farm, Fruitlands, New Harmony, and the Oneida community. Most of these efforts failed because of poor organization, the frequently impractical nature of the participants, and the reluctance of members to accept the standard of living imposed by independent isolation.

For most reformers, however, building God's earthly kingdom meant a concern for better schools, hospitals, and prisons;

movements against liquor, tobacco, cruelty to animals, and war; movements for women's rights and better living for working people; and, finally, opposition to the great evil of human slavery. In countless editorials, propaganda sheets, sermons, speeches, poems, and books, and through associations, societies, and political movements, the work went forward and carried itself to a climax, oddly enough, in a crusade against an institution which did not even exist in the region.

Much of central and western New York was settled by New Englanders, and the same religious and intellectual ferment spread quickly through that region. New York cities came to share the same industrial problems. New York politics were characterized also by struggles between the great harbor city and the rural areas and by struggles between the owners of the big landed estates and the smaller farmers. New York had been one of the least democratic of the American colonies, and the years of conflict spent correcting this situation left the state one of the most democratic in the Union. By the 1840's the Whig party had abandoned its earlier conservative image and was competing with the Jacksonian Democrats for the votes of workingmen as well as liberal reformers. The Whig governor and senator, William H. Seward, and his alter ego, editor Thurlow Weed, adopted first the emotionalism of anti-Masonry and then the rhetoric of antislavery and Free-Soilism in their never-ending struggle against the Democratic party of Martin Van Buren and his successors. As governor, senator, and President, Van Buren was a Jeffersonian agrarian who appealed to farmers with conservative hard-money economics and to workingmen with a powerful democratic ideology. The Whigs served the growing industrial interests, and advocated all the paternalistic federal programs opposed by Van Buren. As Van

The Death of Slavery

Buren's economic principles became less and less applicable to the needs and ambitions of New Yorkers, Seward and Weed found their key to success by adding a new liberal political philosophy. In the end the quest for votes drove many Van Burenites into a partnership with the Whigs in the movement against the extension of slavery.

Pennsylvania was further removed from the unique mind and conscience of New England, and had enjoyed a far more democratic colonial experience than New York. Like New York it was rich in both agricultural and industrial resources. Pennsylvania touched the Great Lakes at its northwestern tip, but it was intimately tied to the southern and middle states by the Ohio River. Andrew Jackson had made the Democratic party a powerful force in Pennsylvania, and, as in New York, the Whigs moved away from political conservatism while working for their traditional aims of high tariff, federal internal improvements, and a United States Bank. Western Pennsylvania was the great hive from which thousands of frontier families had swarmed up and down the valleys, into the South as well as the Northwest. Its people had many ties of kinship in both sections.

Essentially a border state and looking in both directions economically, Pennsylvania was also a state in which the spirit of nationalism burned bright and clear. In general, Pennsylvanians took a tolerant attitude toward their slaveholding brethren, although the Quakers hated the institution itself. It was perhaps no coincidence that Pennsylvania's most important antebellum spokesman and leader was James Buchanan, the peace-seeking compromiser often denounced as a Northern President with Southern principles.

New Jersey shared in the new economic developments of New York and eastern Pennsylvania. The Presbyterian college

18

at Princeton and the Dutch Reformed college called Rutgers helped foster the spirit of John Calvin, but both were less dominated by reforming spirit than Harvard and other New England counterparts. The political parties in New Jersey were fairly evenly matched, but Whig economics dominated.

The Northeast, then, was a varied section characterized by eager acceptance of new technology and by rapid industrialization. It had long since abandoned slavery, but urbanism and industrialization were creating new problems of their own. These in turn were creating in various parts of the region a great age of isms and reforms. The region was caught in something of an inner conflict between the appeal of Democratic political ideology and the desire for Whig economic policies, but the Whig party was doing much to ease this tension by becoming more democratic.

The region had a connection with slavery through the shiploads of Southern cotton which provided raw materials for the textile mills and factories, but slavery and slaveholders were not economic competitors either real or potential. For the Northeast slavery was a distant but all-absorbing evil to be added to the list of dragons against which a generation of reformers had already drawn their swords. The economic and ideological characteristics of the Northeast were destined to set the pattern of the future in American life, and the compulsion to oppose slavery and its extension was certain to spread and gain strength as a result.

The antebellum South was a land of great variety in soils, climate, topography, and economic and social life. Certain general characteristics and problems, however, tended to give it unity. The weather was warm and hence the growing season lasted longer. The rainfall was heavier and more frequent. The soils were in the beginning reasonably fertile, but they were subject to heavy depletion from erosion and excessive one-crop production. The agrarian economic base which supported all the early American colonies lasted long and resisted change in the South because of its success and because of a labor system which became also a social institution. The original shipload of frightened African captives had been increased by 1860 to 4,441,830, of whom 3,838,765 were still slaves in a total Southern population of 11,133,361. An additional 115,000 slaves were also scattered throughout the Northern states.

Slavery was a very important labor system for those engaged in agriculture on any significant scale. It was particularly useful in developing the Southern frontier into a vast cotton kingdom, where the slave's capacity for heavy work in intense heat was put to the maximum use.

The system, however, was expensive and often wasteful. Slaves cost a great deal of money and required subsistence from the cradle to the grave. Large-scale agriculture provided many opportunities for looking busy while doing little, and slavery provided little incentive for conscientious work.

Historians will quarrel forever over the profitability of slavery. The sum total of their efforts to date has been reasonable proof that some people in some parts of the South at certain periods found slavery immensely profitable, whereas for others it was a very heavy economic burden. In 1830 Senator Thomas Hart Benton, who owned or had owned slaves in North Carolina, Tennessee, Virginia, and Missouri, was certain slavery would eventually disappear for economic reasons, and twenty-six years later he had not changed his mind. Benton viewed the difference in race as the only force keeping the institution and the sectional conflict alive.

There Were Sections

The question of profit, however, was purely academic from the viewpoint of most Southerners. Only one Southerner in four owned slaves or had any direct contact with slavery at all. The vast number of non-slaveholding Southerners who supported and thereby made possible the secession and war in 1861 were not offering their lives in defense of slavery because of its profitability.

For slaveholder and non-slaveholder alike, the institution solved the problem of controlling some four million persons of a different color who, through no fault of their own, had been kept for two centuries in a state of captivity, forced labor, and cultural inferiority. In one sense, the slave suffered to an infinitely greater degree the same animosities visited upon the Northern immigrant laborer, but the white immigrant had the immeasurable advantage of being able to disappear through social absorption once he had improved his economic status. The slave had neither education nor property and was denied both. His resulting inferior way of life was then used as a reason for enforcing these prohibitions still further. No one could know just what social and economic convulsions would occur if he should be emancipated, and the speculations concerning such an event were compounded from fear and subconscious guilt and drew heavily upon the frightful race war which had occurred in Haiti at the turn of the century. Fear and rationality are natural enemies, and Southern fears were real enough.

Indeed, any assessment of the profitability of slavery must recognize also its deadening effect upon economic innovation or progress. In seeking to maintain a thriving atmosphere for slavery the South feared and resisted all changes which might weaken the technological and economic basis of the system. And for that matter many parts of the South have continued throughout the century since Appomattox to resist desperately needed progress which might also weaken the bonds of extra-legal inferiority pressed upon the former slave and his descendants since the Civil War. The blinding of Southern eyes and the setting of the Southern mind against the realities of the modern world ultimately cost the South more than all the profits ever made by slavery.

Brazil, where slavery was an economic institution almost divorced from racial implications, abandoned the institution without conflict. The United States, with far more liberal and humane political and social traditions, could not make the same peaceful transition. This fact merely adds to the evidence that slavery as a social rather than an economic institution was the heart of the civilization Southerners were prepared to die for in 1861. Had the slave been white, or had Americans shared the racial unconcern of their Brazilian neighbors, there would have been no American Civil War.

In response to Northern attacks the South ultimately turned to Genesis and to amateur anthropology in defense of slavery. The factor which probably did most to ease Southern consciences, however, was the basic economic security provided for most slaves. Reasonable kindness, however condescending, came naturally to most Southerners, as it did to most Americans everywhere. And beyond these considerations, to mistreat or neglect a slave was to mistreat or neglect an enormous financial investment. The well-treated, well-fed, reasonably happy slave was of infinitely greater value than one requiring constant supervision, policing, or medical care. The usual slave diet was monotonous, but it was more adequate than that of most laboring people in the mid-nineteenth century world. In most cases, also, it was shared by the young and old as well as the produc-

There Were Sections

tive. Slave housing was crude and often dirty, but usually dry. Masters and slaves alike endured the same atrocious medical treatment, but they shared equally in the best available. Southerners never tired of comparing the security and stability of slave life to the frequent poverty, unemployment, and general misery of many free laborers in the American Northeast as well as abroad. Also, the extremely limited opportunities available to free Negroes in many Northern as well as Southern states enabled Southerners to make numerous comparisons between the happy existence enjoyed by slaves and the misery endured by former slaves who had gained their freedom.

This security plus adequate time and opportunity for sexual activity apparently did keep a majority of the slaves at least acquiescent, just as the same elements have often kept other large populations living placidly under the most stultifying political dictatorships.

For those members of any society who prefer the responsibilities of self-direction, however, slavery is obviously a frightful way of life. By its very security and by its severe limitations upon the achievement of his potential as a human being, slavery robbed the slave of the right to worry and to dream. Enforced illiteracy may be a minor imposition upon those uninterested in reading, but its impact upon a gifted mind can hardly be measured. Likewise, the narrow horizons that provide satisfactory vistas for some can be dungeon walls for those with initiative and curiosity. Perhaps only those who have been moved to explore continents, oceans, skies, and the great scientific mysteries can fully understand the tragedy of those forbidden to explore beyond the next hill.

The intelligent male slave on one of the relatively few large plantations might aspire to the status of a minor overseer, mechanic, artisan, or coachman. He might even become a personal body servant or valet. On extremely rare occasions a talented slave might even be permitted to carve statuary and other decorations for the master's house, but the names of such artists were not bequeathed to posterity. The female slave of ability might become a personal maid, chambermaid, or nursemaid, and, rarely, through personal relations with the family she might with the passing of the years assume the character of a "mammy," entrusted with unusual authority and responsibility. Even these limited positions, however, were far beyond the hopes of the average slave.

More obvious were the evils stressed by Northern critics. They were not common, but they were always possible and they did occur. Slaves could be whipped and otherwise cruelly mistreated despite protective laws and the pressures of public opinion. Husbands, wives, and children could be separated by sale. The laws of marriage were not mandatory, and licentiousness for the sole purpose of providing new slaves for the market could be encouraged. Comelier females could be subjected to the whims of masters and overseers. In a nation dedicated in theory at least to the essential value of every individual, even one of these occurrences made slavery a relic of barbarism.

And finally, if power has a corrupting influence, then surely the absolute ownership of other men was an unholy devil gnawing at the otherwise rational, humane, and civilized instincts of a great many Southerners. The strident demands of Southern leaders for slave rights in territories where no slaveholder intended to go, and the unreal Southern arguments for secession in the face of Northern assurances that slavery would not be disturbed, were part of a mentality conditioned at least in part by the very nature of slavery. The delusions of grandeur

There Were Sections

which led some Southerners to visualize a great Southern slave empire encompassing the Caribbean, Mexico, and Central America were cut from the same cloth. In addition to economic interest and genuine fears of a convulsive racial conflict, the simple fear of losing a status of power and inherent superiority over large numbers of other people was a significant part of the Southern attachment to slavery and remains part of the present pattern of discrimination. The arguments of John C. Calhoun to the contrary, slavery did not create a higher breed of humanity among the master race.

The generation of Southerners who fought and died because of slavery, however, did not create their curse. Whatever its advantages or evils, and whatever the motivations of its defenders, slavery was at bottom a terrible problem long since bred into their society and intimately involved with its most vital parts. Like surgery, its excision by any means was certain to be both painful and dangerous, and there were no precedents to indicate with any certainty what the results would be. The Southerners of 1861 were the victims as well as the defenders of their peculiar institution.

The slaveholders who abhorred the worst practices of the system resented the implication that these were universal and sought increasingly to identify all that was good in Southern life with slavery. The non-slaveholding small farmers, small businessmen, teachers, preachers, clerks, lawyers, and white laborers, many of them desperately poor, who made up three-fourths of the Southern population knew only that the end of slavery could have calamitous possibilities. Some still aspired to be slaveholders. Countless others feared the economic and social competition of the slave. Many could be moved to terror by the picture of violence, chaos, and bloodshed conjured up by vote-hunting politicians. By 1861 they were ready to fight for a plantation type of civilization in which less than 3 per cent of the Southern people actually shared.

In politics Southern Democrats were Jeffersonian in outlook. They opposed the protective tariffs which raised the prices they must pay and reduced the markets for Southern crops abroad. They objected to federally financed internal improvements which might deplete the treasury and create a necessity for higher tariffs. They applauded Andrew Jackson's war on the United States Bank and distrusted the Northern banking and business community in general.

To make these economic issues a vital part of the sectional conflict, however, is to ignore the enormous strength of the Southern Whig party until the party was destroyed by the slavery quarrel in the 1850's. As Charles Sellers has shown, the Whig party in the slave states actually enjoyed a slight edge over the Democrats in both presidential and congressional elections in the 1830's and 1840's. Also, the Southern Whig congressmen on the whole supported the same commercial, industrial, and financial interests and policies as their Northern Whig colleagues. The antebellum South had its powerful urban commercial and banking interests too, and a majority of the great planters followed their lead in politics. The ancient myth of the South's provoking war and defeat by its united opposition to economic policies needed by Northern businessmen has lived too long. There were as many former Whigs, including Confederate Vice-President Alexander H. Stephens and Secretary of War Judah P. Benjamin, as there were Democrats in the ranks of secession in 1861.

In the end, however, the fiercely competing economic and political interests which had given the South a healthy two-party system and had kept the region in a lively turmoil for years finally formed a united front in defense of slavery and the right to extend it to new territories. No other issue could have achieved this result.

The Southwest differed in many ways from the Southeast, but in the end the common denominator of slavery drew them together as one section. The Northwest, however, remained in many ways distinct from the Northeast. The great region composed of Ohio, Indiana, Illinois, Wisconsin, and Michigan, and later Iowa and Minnesota, provided the spark of nationalism which held the Union together. In 1861 northeastern abolitionists like William Lloyd Garrison and Horace Greeley were willing for the erring Southern sisters to depart in peace. Abraham Lincoln of Illinois, however, speaking for his own section, could not allow the great American experiment in democracy to be split apart by secession.

The earliest settlers in the Northwest were largely Southerners. By 1830 there were nearly 700,000 former Southerners in the area, and they still equaled all other groups in 1850. Tens of thousands of Scotch-Irish, Welsh, and German frontiersmen had started from the great melting pot of western Pennsylvania and had briefly settled in North Carolina, Tennessee, Kentucky, and points even further south before slowly emigrating back northward into southern Ohio, Illinois, and Indiana. The Southerners believed that land that wouldn't grow trees wouldn't grow crops either, and as a result most of them picked land with trees and water. They ignored the rich but tough-sodded prairies and spent countless laborious hours chopping out the timber. The prairies were left for a later generation of New Englanders, who quickly invented adequate plows.

The Death of Slavery

These and other factors, including proximity to the South, tended to place Southerners on lands untouched by the glaciers, although forests also grew on unglaciated land. Frederick Jackson Turner once marked a map of the Northwest in different colors to show the glaciated and unglaciated land. He then marked with the same colors another map showing the areas which had voted for Abraham Lincoln and for Stephen A. Douglas in 1860. The patterns were almost identical. Lincoln the Kentuckian had moved to Illinois to become the hero of the New England element, while Douglas from Vermont had become the idol of the Illinois upland Southerners.

The Southern immigrants were mostly plain cabin people who loved to cut down trees, fired long rifles with rare skill, were often intemperate, and were still oftener illiterate. They enjoyed moving, and the covered wagon was always ready for loading at the word of better pickings in a new location. Some carried a few books and advocated education. Medical care was primitive, and death was omnipresent. Their folksongs and hymns, naturally enough, were frequently mournful sagas of family tragedy and hopes for future reunions in a better world. In their religion and in political attitudes they were often highly emotional.

In 1861 many of this group, particularly in the Ohio River valley, remained sympathetic to their Southern brethren. Still more, however, had but few kind memories of their former slaveholding competitors. Often intolerant toward the slaves and freed Negroes, they were also violently opposed to any extension of slavery, and they bitterly resented the possibility that an independent South might cut their river route to New Orleans.

After 1830 a new wave of immigration poured into the

There Were Sections

Northwest from the Northeast. Indeed, New England would have been almost stripped of its population except for the new European immigrants thronging the harbors. Fleeing from agricultural depressions and urban industrial problems, and seeking the new opportunities offered by a rich frontier, New Englanders and other northeasterners came out in Great Lakes steamers, in covered wagons, on horseback, and on foot. New England towns, with their town squares, Congregationalist churches, and little Yales and Harvards, sprang up everywhere, until western New York, northern Ohio, Indiana, and Illinois, and parts of Michigan and Wisconsin, became virtually a greater New England.

These travelers were generally concerned with education and a more intellectual brand of religion. New Englanders frequently moved in entire communities after drawing up Mayflower-type compacts which not only listed the rules of membership, but also emphasized their reasons for moving in religious terms. Many New Englanders considered the West a great heathen area to be rescued for God's kingdom, and glorified their own quest for a new fortune accordingly. Their sense of religious mission was a comfort in the midst of hardship and danger, and it developed easily into a strong sense of national mission later. Such people ultimately opposed slavery not only as unchristian and undemocratic, but also as a barrier to the achievement of God's plan for America.

A third varied population group was also important. Immigrants from England, Ireland, Germany, and Scandinavia came in large numbers to escape various ills in Europe. The generation which came after the unsuccessful European revolutions of 1848 added a group short in numbers, but long in quality and devotion to democratic principles. To those who had fled from

29

oppression as well as famine, the very word slavery was anathema. The spirit of nationalism and a willingness to defend their new nation against those who would divide it settled upon the new Americans easily but firmly.

In areas where the different groups intermingled, the adjustment occasionally took time. Southerners who hung clothes on bushes and worried little about boundaries learned to live with New Englanders who used clotheslines and made careful surveys. In Wisconsin the New England puritans had to adjust their blue laws to the habits of Germans who liked beer and Beethoven on Sundays and Irishmen prepared for any amusement on any day. Yankee religion had to compete with the simpler fundamentalist beliefs of the frontier revivalists, and mixed congregations were occasionally treated to furious debates between hellfire-and-brimstone practitioners and their more restrained competitors and brethren.

Like the other sections, however, the Northwest had certain unifying features despite the infinite variety of its land and people. Although numerous towns were approaching the status of cities by 1861, and each town had its merchants and capitalists, the overwhelming majority of the people were small independent farmers. Farmers wanted land, and new population meant economic progress for everyone. The demand for cheap or free government land was, therefore, almost universal. Senator Thomas Hart Benton of the border state of Missouri spoke for Southwest and Northwest alike when he pronounced the right to own land a natural right—an obvious corollary to life, liberty, and the pursuit of happiness.

Westerners, likewise, had a virtual mania for internal improvements like roads, bridges, canals, river and lake channels, and harbors at federal expense. A convention at St. Louis in

There Were Sections

1840 defined the Mississippi River from its mouth to its source as an inland harbor, and argued that as such it should be cleared of snags and sandbars for its entire length. The northwestern states incurred huge debts for such purposes, and often had difficulty choosing between Benton's program for reducing the price of public land and Henry Clay's plan for maintaining prices while distributing the money thus collected to the states for internal improvements.

On the questions of tariffs and banking the Northwest was divided. Enough northwesterners joined with Southerners to pass the low tariff bills of 1846 and 1857, but others were furiously angry over certain provisions in both. In general, westerners everywhere wanted all the paper money and credit they could find anywhere. They rejoiced at the inflation which followed President Jackson's war on the United States Bank, but promptly deserted Jackson's hand-picked successor, Van Buren, when the latter sought to take the government entirely out of the banking business and adopted hard-money, deflationary policies in general.

Westerners everywhere liked the rugged personality of Andrew Jackson and the antiaristocratic democratic philosophy of equal opportunity preached by his followers. The hard money and laissez-faire economic principles of the Jacksonian inner circle were far less popular, however. In 1840, when the Whigs themselves went democratic with log cabins, hard cider, and the old soldier William Henry Harrison, westerners gleefully helped vote the Democrats out of office.

In the 1840's the Democrats recovered much of their old strength in the Northwest by becoming the party of territorial expansion. Also, just as the Whigs were becoming more democratic in outlook and image, northwestern Democrats like

The Death of Slavery

Stephen A. Douglas and others were becoming more and more Whiggish in their economic posture. By 1849 Democrats Douglas and Benton were vying with each other in demands that the federal government finance the building of the transcontinental railroads, and Douglas was later responsible for the initial appropriation for the Illinois Central Railroad.

By 1850, however, northwesterners had developed a powerful animosity towards the South and its peculiar institution. When President Polk chose to fight for Texas and California, but compromised on the boundary of Oregon, many westerners felt betrayed. The lower tariff of 1846 and the restoration of the independent treasury were unpopular with others. Polk's veto of river and harbor legislation, and subsequent opposition to homestead laws by the "pro-Southern" Northern Presidents Pierce and Buchanan added to the picture.

Men who felt they were building a greater America and developing a continent for democracy and Christianity often came to identify their wishes and policies with God's will. Southern opposition was regarded as a barrier to human progress and the growth and well-being of America as ordained by the Almighty himself. Naturally enough, also, Southern perversity was attributed largely to the corrupting influence of slavery. In northwestern language "slavocracy" was more than a term to describe a group supporting an inhumane institution. It became the symbol for a decadent aristocracy blocking the efforts of men who did their own work to expand and develop America into the nation it should be. Men from states with laws excluding free Negroes from their borders became the most implacable foes of slavery, and were ready to believe any charge, however unjustified, that the South was plotting to force slavery upon areas further west and would not hesitate to impose it on free states also if given the opportunity.

There were sections in the America of 1860, but each section contained many diverse elements, and the usual generalizations about any section are subject to serious qualifications. Americans everywhere had much in common, and among their institutions only slavery was unique. The Southern farmer with one or two slaves or perhaps a family of slaves, however, had more in common with the Northern small farmer than he did with the great plantation owner. And, as John C. Calhoun was quick to point out, the Northern factory owner shared many of the employer problems of the planter. By 1860, however, the dominant Southern leadership considered the other sections a mortal threat escapable only by secession. And in the act of seceding the South did in fact become a mortal threat to the American Union, a national state for which the non-slave sections were prepared to fight and die.

III

"If the Republic Must Be Blotted Out..."

If the State cannot survive the anti-slavery agitation, then let the State perish. If the Church must be cast down by the strugglings of humanity to be free, then let the church fall, . . . If the American Union cannot be maintained, except by immolating human freedom on the altar of tyranny, then let the American Union be consumed by a living thunderbolt, and no tear be shed over its ashes. If the Republic must be blotted out from the roll of nations, by proclaiming liberty to the captives, then let the Republic sink beneath the waves of oblivion, . . .

WILLIAM LLOYD GARRISON

A budding Southern movement against slavery at the time of the American Revolution was checked by the inability of anti-slavery Southerners like Washington, Jefferson, and Randolph to imagine an acceptable alternative, and Eli Whitney's cotton gin soon gave the institution a new economic strength. Still, however, antislavery newspapers sprang up in several Southern cities, and strong minorities argued eloquently for abolition in the constitutional conventions of both Virginia and Tennessee. Likewise, the ill-fated American Colonization Society, which recognized the racial barrier to emancipation, began in the South. In 1822, however, the alleged attempt of Denmark Vesey, a talented South Carolina mulatto preacher, to plan an insurrection led to the hanging of Vesey and thirty-four followers. The Vesey conspiracy probably existed only in inflamed white imaginations, but Southerners everywhere were horrified. This fear was renewed in 1831, when Nat Turner led some Virginia slaves in a revolt which cost the lives of more than fifty persons. These events, plus the rising volume of antislavery criticism from the North, ended the Southern antislavery movements forever.

Southerners, however, who moved north and west by the hundreds of thousands, usually took with them a deep-seated hatred of slavery. The great majority sought freedom from the stultifying economic competition of slavery, and usually remained racists with no desire whatever to see Southern slaves free to come northward. Some, however, left because they could not bear living where they had to watch the evils of slavery and act as though they approved. Abolitionists like James G. Birney, Edward Coles, Levi Coffin, John Rankin, the Grimké sisters, the Dickey brothers, Samuel Crothers, Gideon Blackburn, William T. Allen, and James A. Thome—to name only a few—were all transplanted Southerners.

It was both natural and inevitable that an antislavery movement should sweep through the Northeast and spread to the Northwest in the 1830's and 1840's. It was an age of reform, and slavery was clearly the most flagrant violation of the

The Death of Slavery

Sermon on the Mount and the Declaration of Independence to be found in America. Also, it was far away and could be attacked with an impunity not always enjoyed when combating evils nearer at hand. New Englanders in bitter conflict with each other on local matters could share a common antipathy toward slavery. Indeed, some found antislavery a useful channel into which otherwise dangerous emotions could be harmlessly diverted. Local defenders of long hours and low wages in northeastern factories resented Southern opposition to their favorite economic programs in Congress and found it easy to tolerate and even share the attacks on Southern slavery.

The motivations and characteristics of the Northern abolitionists were varied and complex enough to provide later historians with a wealth of controversy. The abolitionists were heroes for decades until the terrible results of twentieth-century fanaticism brought a new regard for compromise and new analyses stressing the faults, inconsistencies, and intolerance of the abolitionists. They were a prime target for the revisionist historians, and many of the criticisms were valid. The civil rights struggle of the 1950's and 1960's, however, has brought a new regard for their work, at least in Northern intellectual circles.

It has been argued successively that the abolitionists were driven by only the purest Christian virtues; that because of neurotic tendencies induced by personal frustration, they were intolerant, humorless, and vituperative, and that they attacked slavery as a substitute for an unfair world; that they were really displaced middle-income aristocrats striking back at a world dominated by the new leaders of commerce, finance, and industry; and that in fact, most of them were successful, happy, well-adjusted persons. The fact that most of them were Whigs in opposition to the democracy of Andrew Jackson is also cited to show their lack of genuine humanitarian concern. Whether the truly effective center of abolition was the Northeast or the Old Northwest has also been ardently debated, while some have argued that the northwestern abolitionists were either transplanted New Englanders or derived their ideas from the same holy source of religious principle. Still others have gone a step backward to England to find the true origins of the movement.

Suffice to say that the evidence supports all of these contentions. Garrison was neurotic and spoke in the accents of hatred. John Brown was criminally insane. Parker, Phillips, Beecher, and Gerrit Smith were dedicated but wholly intolerant. Weld, the Grimké sisters, and many of the Quakers were genuinely humanitarian Christians; Tappan, Emerson, and Dana fretted at the onslaught of modern industrialism; fifty-nine of sixty Massachusetts abolitionists were Whigs; and Lowell, Whittier, and Longfellow were apparently supremely happy men. The personalities of the nameless thousands who followed them cannot be analyzed, but it may be assumed that the same variety ran entirely through the movement.

Whatever their character, the abolitionists were never more than a tiny minority of the whole people. Indeed, until well into the 1840's, most of them were proscribed by their own churches, even in New England. Moses Stuart, professor of Hebrew at Andover Theological Seminary, justified slavery from the Old Testament. President Lord of Dartmouth argued that slavery was an institution of God, and Episcopal Bishop Hopkins of Vermont was no less a fervent defender of slavery. Theodore Parker's colleagues would not exchange pulpits with him. The Methodist General Conference of 1838 censured two of its members who had spoken for abolition, and the New York Methodist Conference of the same year warned its members not to read the antislavery paper *Zion's Watchman*. By 1850 the abolition societies claimed a total membership of 150,000, but those members active enough to be remembered number fewer than 250.

The abolitionist who had the greatest sustained impact upon the South was clearly William Lloyd Garrison, whose rabid demands for immediate emancipation regardless of the cost won but few Northern followers. Abandoned by a drunken father and condemned to a miserable childhood, Garrison reached manhood steeped in anger at an unfair and unjust world. After a harsh apprenticeship as a printer and writer, Garrison finally became editor of the *National Philanthropist*, a newspaper dedicated to the suppression of intemperance and other vices of the less godly. Editor Garrison soon added lotteries, sabbath-breaking, and war to his list of enemies. Then he was invited to help Benjamin Lundy edit an abolition paper in Baltimore. At Jonesboro, Tennessee, Lundy had earlier published one of America's earliest abolition papers. In Baltimore Garrison was jailed and mistreated.

Overnight Garrison abandoned gradual emancipation and called for abolition immediately and by force and violence if necessary. In 1830 he founded *The Liberator* in Boston and announced: "*I do not wish to think or speak or write with moderation. I will not retreat a single inch, and I will be heard.*" To Garrison the problem was a simple one of right and wrong. Slavery violated Christianity and the Declaration of Independence. If the Constitution protected slavery, then this "League with Death and agreement with Hell" should be destroyed, and Garrison illustrated his point by burning a copy of the Constitution over a candle while his audience breathed a fervent

"If the Republic Must Be Blotted Out . . ."

"Amen." To Garrison slaveholders were no better than criminals and deserved no protection or consideration whatever. Slavery must be abolished regardless of any cost in bloodshed and suffering.

Small wonder that Southerners, whether slaveholders or not, were frightened by the doctrines of Garrison, and small wonder that Garrison's Northern following was never very numerous. The circulation of *The Liberator* was never more than three thousand, but Southern editors regularly reprinted his insults and attacks.

Southern policies of the immediate antebellum period were clearly dictated by fear, pride, and emotion rather than a rational calculation of self-interest, and much of the responsibility for this must be laid to Garrison. In the end he helped frighten the South into self-destructive actions far more dangerous to the South and to slavery than any actions seriously contemplated by either the leaders or the people of the Northern states. With the possible exception of John Brown, no one ever quite equaled the position of Garrison in Southern minds as the stereotype example of the Yankee enemy.

The man who did the most to make abolition respectable and who won by far the most converts was Theodore Dwight Weld. Weld preached gradual emancipation, to begin immediately and to be accomplished within the existing constitutional and political framework. Weld's program did not suggest war and bloodshed, and did not threaten or heap abuse upon the state, the church, or the white Southerners. Although Garrison ultimately adopted a pacifist philosophy which excused him from direct action of any sort, he established his reputation with the loudly proclaimed principle that the end justified any means. Weld preached no such doctrine.

Converted to religion by the great Christian Perfectionist,

The Death of Slavery

Charles G. Finney, Weld became an abolitionist on the basis of Christian principle. By 1832 he was a somewhat mature student at Lane Theological Seminary in Cincinnati, where he organized a series of debates on the twin subjects of abolition and colonization.

The president of Lane was Lyman Beecher, a well-known New England theologian. Beecher's daughter Harriet was destined to write *Uncle Tom's Cabin,* and his son Henry Ward would become an abolitionist after whom frontier Free Soilers would name their rifles "Beecher's Bibles."

In 1832, however, the elder Beecher was far less bold. He bowed to local pressures and ordered the debates stopped even though abolitionists were among the institution's chief contributors. More than fifty students led by Weld resigned, and most of them ultimately moved northward to Oberlin, a small church college founded the year before by John T. Shipherd and Philo Stewart. Under the influence of Asa Mahan, John Morgan, Weld, and Finney, and with financial aid from men like Arthur Tappan, Oberlin became a great radiating center of Christian Perfectionism, social reform, and abolitionism. Among the institution's earliest heresies was the admission of both Negroes and women to full academic equality, and its tradition of academic freedom remains unsurpassed. As might have been expected, the college also became an important station on the Underground Railroad.

With Oberlin as one of his bases, Weld in good biblical fashion trained seventy disciples to go forth and spread the gospel of God's objections to slavery. At first the seventy were suppressed, insulted, and occasionally manhandled. On March 3, 1837, a young Illinois legislator named Abraham Lincoln expressed a widely held view: "The institution of slavery is founded on both injustice and bad policy, but . . . the promulgation of abolition doctrines tends rather to increase than abate its evils." By peaceful but dedicated perseverance, however, Weld's apostles slowly won forbearance and then respect.

Meanwhile, Weld joined Garrison, the Tappan brothers, and others in the American Anti-Slavery Society. The society printed and circulated antislavery tracts by the thousands, while Weld and his group took the lead in gathering thousands of signatures for petitions asking Congress to abolish slavery in the District of Columbia. If gradual emancipation were to begin immediately, where better than in the District, where Congress was the only government and where no state laws protecting slavery existed?

The petition movement was a stroke of genius. At this point the abolitionists were still a tiny group generally regarded as crackpots. The struggle in Congress over the petitions, however, gave their movement a new base and a new appeal. The sacred right of petition could not be threatened without rousing the anger of Americans almost everywhere. Yet the South's most prominent leader found a resistance to the right of petition itself to be politically expedient. Weld and his great supporter, John Quincy Adams, found an inadvertent ally in John C. Calhoun, but this cannot be fully understood without a close look at the politics of the young American nation.

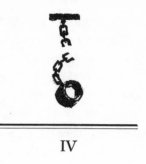

IV

Democracy and Its Leaders

By the mid-1830's American politicians had developed a new set of motivations, and were becoming more and more aware of the value of emotional appeals often unrelated to genuine issues.

Jacksonian Democracy had come to America in the wake of an ever-expanding electorate, and it had brought with it the principle of giving the jobs and favors to the faithful of the victorious party. As government grew in size at every level from town council to the federal executive departments, elections became more and more important to more and more people for reasons often unrelated to contending principles and national policies. The competition for power and influence remained for some a struggle between philosophies and programs. For some it also became an economic profession. For still others it became a gigantic sport with prestige, power,

42

and the sheer joy of victory as the rewards. For all too many, issues had become weapons to be sought out, managed, and utilized in the endless quest for votes among the body politic.

In short, the United States had achieved a democracy ideally suited for reasonably wise and just decision-making where none of the alternatives posed any mortal threat to the real or imagined interests of any particular group or section. The system was also destined to function magnificently even in crises threatening the very existence of the Republic when the major problem was an easily identified external enemy. But it was not a system designed to handle peacefully a question like slavery unless the political leadership on both sides should rise above the temptations offered by such an issue.

If politics was a full-time profession for many, it was a major participation sport for almost everyone. Americans were a competitive people, and the almost continuous political contests filled a void to be crammed to overflowing in later years by radio, television, movies, and nationally organized athletics. In taverns, inns, hotels, stores, blacksmith shops, and courthouses—indeed, anywhere men could be found—Americans argued and quarreled incessantly over candidates and issues. European travelers were astounded at the vigorous arguments and assumption of absolute knowledge of the widest variety of political subjects by unlettered citizens in every village, hamlet, and farmhouse.

The fountains of knowledge were the local newspapers and a handful of papers and magazines national in scope, almost all of which were openly allied with one political party or the other and often with one leader or faction of that party. Editors exchanged subscriptions and copied, supported, and disputed each others' news and views. National papers like the Democratic *Washington Globe* and *New York Evening Post* and the Whig *National Intelligencer, Chicago Tribune,* and *New York Tribune* fed news and editorials to their satellites in the same fashion as a modern press service. Although large sections of the proceedings in Congress were reported verbatim, most editors saw fit to minimize or limit what Francis P. Blair called "the stale and worn-out speeches" of the opposition. Both the *Globe* and the *Intelligencer* printed and distributed by the thousands the more effective speeches of their favorite leaders. Copies of newspapers and magazines circulated from hand to hand and were read by far more people than their subscription lists would indicate.

An unfortunate accompaniment of this essentially healthy interest in politics was an addiction to violence in many parts of the country. A people who had spent so many years shooting Indians and animals and who had written the right of every individual to bear arms into their national Constitution found violent personal conflicts easy to forgive if the antagonists had a theoretically even chance to kill or maim each other. Judges and juries alike were remarkably lenient to the victors of fatal encounters, and in numerous states dueling itself was still legal.

While criminal violence abounded in the poorer areas of the great northeastern cities, it was primarily in the South and West that both politicians and editors found their professions dangerous. Andrew Jackson carried a varied assortment of lead in his thin, weary body. Thomas Hart Benton, in addition to his pistol fight with Jackson, had killed a man in a duel at nine feet, with this point-blank distance set by Benton to offset a complaint that his marksmanship was superior. Representative Spencer Pettis and Major Thomas Biddle, brother of Nicholas Biddle, killed each other in a five-foot duel, with this suicidal

44

range set by Biddle to compensate for his nearsightedness. Representative Cilley of Maine was killed by Representative Graves of Kentucky in a rifle duel which Cilley had done his best to avoid. Happily, a duel between Henry Clay and John Randolph ended harmlessly. Daniel Webster was intelligent enough to refuse a challenge from Randolph and fortunate to represent a state which put no premium on recklessness or marksmanship. Sam Houston gave his congressional colleague Stansberry a frightful thrashing on a Washington street. Editor Francis P. Blair carried a pistol and avoided duels in part because of his reputation for marksmanship. Blair's competitor Duff Green, who worshiped at the Calhoun shrine, did fight duels and once received a terrible beating at the hands of South Carolina unionist James Blair. In Frankfort, Kentucky, editor Thomas Benning was killed in cold blood by Charles Wickliffe, who was himself later killed in a duel by Benning's successor. Editor J. H. Pleasants of Richmond, who once threatened Francis P. Blair, was killed by Thomas Ritchie, Jr., son of Pleasants' rival editor in Richmond. Accounts of such incidents could be multiplied many times.

Obviously, the great majority of politicians and editors did not get involved in mayhem, but the public tolerance of violence was probably an important factor in the coming of the American Civil War. The all too frequent translation of political disagreement and rivalry into personal hatred and physical conflict made the realistic appraisal of emotional issues more difficult. A traditional indifference to violence also helped keep both Southerners and Northerners unaware of the frightful extremities a military solution of their difficulties would reach. Southerners really believed their boast that any of their number could whip ten Yankees, and this notion contributed not a little to their incredibly light-hearted and optimistic approach to the question of war.

The politician who used the slavery issue most consistently if not always most effectively for his own ends was John C. Calhoun of South Carolina. Puritanical, humorless, and self-righteous, Calhoun usually translated his own ambitions and problems into matters of universal significance, and he commanded a fanatical devotion among his followers. Calhoun has fascinated and won high praise from the historians of the South and the North alike, and his place in history has grown in importance from the American tendency to view the heroes of lost causes with feelings of sportsmanlike sympathy. Only when his most cherished premises are examined in minute detail and when the full scale of twists and turns in his career is traced do cracks in the traditional Calhoun image begin to appear.

In 1812 the young Calhoun was a war hawk determined to punish Britain and liberate Canada. In succeeding years he was a great nationalist and supported both the protective tariff and the United States Bank. As Secretary of War under President Monroe, Calhoun was one of the five candidates for President in 1824 but withdrew to become the vice-presidential candidate on both the Adams and Jackson tickets. In 1828 he again accepted the second place after apparently being persuaded that the ailing Andrew Jackson could last but one term at best.

In 1828 Calhoun was certain he would be the next President, but his path to the White House was suddenly blocked by unforeseen circumstances. Old Hickory's beloved wife Rachel had died, reportedly from shock caused by the vicious and untrue stories circulated during the campaign about the circumstances of her marriage to Jackson. Unable to save Rachel and heartbroken by her death, Jackson arrived in Washington just in time to discover a similar situation involving his new Secretary of War, John Eaton. Eaton had married a young widow of questionable repute, and the other administration wives, at least partly from jealousy of her good looks, were soon pointedly ignoring her parties and not inviting her to theirs. There is evidence also that pro-Calhoun men in the cabinet hoped thereby to drive Eaton out because Eaton was one of the few cabinet members devoted to Calhoun's chief rival for the succession, Secretary of State Martin Van Buren.

Andrew Jackson promptly made Mrs. Eaton's cause his own and pronounced her "pure as the driven snow." In this squabble, the aristocratic Mrs. Calhoun was ostentatiously on the side of Mrs. Eaton's enemies, while Van Buren, a widower, was free to attend Mrs. Eaton publicly and spend long hours with his fellow widower, Jackson, in conversations about the wickedness of female gossip.

Also, when Calhoun's friends, including Duff Green, editor of the administration newspaper, began to push the Carolinian's claims for a presidential nomination in 1832, Van Buren's friends realized that the iron-willed Jackson would live through another term and longer if he so decided. Soon they produced correspondence which showed that Calhoun as Secretary of War had suggested a court-martial for Jackson at the time of Old Hickory's invasion of Florida in 1818. Already angered by the Eaton affair, Jackson demanded an explanation which Calhoun could not provide, and their break was complete. After the election of 1832 Calhoun resigned from the vice-presidency and returned to South Carolina to be elected to the Senate.

Finding himself in open conflict with Jackson, the full extent of whose invincible popularity was not yet fully clear in 1830,

The Death of Slavery

Calhoun turned to South Carolina and the other Southern states for a new political base. In 1828 he had already penned anonymously his doctrine of nullification because of South Carolina's anger over the tariff. In this document he had argued persuasively that ultimate sovereignty rested in the states rather than in the federal government, and that any state could declare federal laws unconstitutional and refuse to obey them. If three-fourths of the states, meeting in conventions, should rule the law in question constitutional, it would indeed be so, inasmuch as three-fourths of the states have the power to amend the Constitution. Otherwise, however, the disobedience or "nullification" should stand. Even if three-fourths of the states should make the law valid, the nullifying state should still have a choice between submission and secession.

Nullification was directed against the tariff. Andrew Jackson was personally a low tariff man and a slaveholding Southern planter, and his land policies were calculated to fill the treasury and render the high tariff both unnecessary and inexpedient. Henry Clay was virtually the father of the protective tariff, but in the election of 1832 Calhoun and his friends opposed Jackson, the only candidate who could defeat Clay. Jackson's election, said Duff Green's *Telegraph*, would enable "daring and corrupt politicians" to "subvert the very foundations of liberty, and convert this government into the corrupt engine of the most odious and profligate despotism."

In 1832 Americans elected a Congress which by all contemporary accounts was low tariff in sentiment. The horse and water transportation of those years, however, dictated that the Congress chosen in 1832 would not take office until December, 1833. The other low tariff states were prepared to wait calmly for a peaceful solution in their favor, but Calhoun was unwilling to see the issue settled so easily. Congress met in December, 1832, to receive the stern announcement by President Jackson that South Carolina was attempting to disobey a federal law. A substantial naval force was already en route to Charleston, and Congress was soon debating an authorization for the use of force, which Old Hickory clearly intended to use whether the bill passed or not. In the end the crisis was resolved with a compromise tariff which provided for a gradual reduction of the tariff over a ten year period to a 20 per cent level and thereby put the question off limits for succeeding Congresses until 1842. For the rest of his life Henry Clay credited Calhoun with saving the tariff in 1833.

The compromise was hardly a Southern victory. The act of 1832 had eliminated the tariff on the cheap woolens worn by almost all Southern slaves. The compromise tariff of 1833 restored this duty to 50 per cent and also provided for evaluations at the port of entry rather than the port of departure—a provision which added the cost of transportation to the base value for taxation.

The best hope for the high tariff was the possibility that the national treasury could be emptied by 1842, since low tariffs were the natural product of a full treasury. In 1835, however, Calhoun originated a program for giving the surplus funds from the national treasury to the states. In 1836 this plan became law in the guise of a "deposit" bill which decreed that the money was to be returnable immediately upon demand. The states received and quickly spent more than $23,000,000, and the federal government still has a lien against the states that spent it. This venture and some other mishaps reduced the $36,000,000 surplus of 1836 to a deficit of $12,000,000 by the end of 1837. A new revenue tariff was absolutely essential by 1842.

The Death of Slavery

Having opposed the Democratic administration as long as it was headed by the slaveholding Tennessee planter, Calhoun promptly rejoined his old party when Jackson was replaced by the essentially far more libertarian New Yorker, Martin Van Buren. With no visible pain, Calhoun switched from support of the United States Bank to advocating the independent treasury program of Van Buren, and he joined his old enemy Thomas Hart Benton in stopping the final treasury payment to the states.

After Van Buren's defeat in 1840, Calhoun saw more new light. After an internal improvements convention at Memphis he discovered that the Mississippi river was "a great inland sea," and began to advocate internal improvements at federal expense. He also promised northeastern industrialists that he would support a tariff in exchange for their help in reaching the White House, and he reiterated his earlier arguments that employers of free and slave labor alike should be united against any show of independence by their workers. Northeastern industrialists and Southern planters should stand together against the common enemy, said Calhoun, because men who were menial laborers, whether white or black, slave or free, had neither the capacity for nor the right to equality or liberty. Slavery, said Calhoun, was "the most safe and stable basis for free institutions in the world. It is impossible with us that conflict can take place between labor and capital which makes it so difficult to establish and maintain free institutions throughout the wealthy and highly civilized nations where such institutions as ours do not exist."

When antislavery pamphlets appeared in the Southern mails in 1835, Calhoun demanded unsuccessfully that Congress forbid their delivery. When the petitions for abolition in the District began to flood Congress, most of the members urged that the petitions be accepted and promptly tabled without discussion. Calhoun, however, insisted that the petitions be rejected to show that Congress had no constitutional power on the subject. The result was the first congressional debate over slavery, a debate in which the abolitionists were pushed by Calhoun into the highly respectable role of defenders of the sacred right of petition. Almost alone, Calhoun turned the petitions into a major issue and set about to project further his own image as the South's great defender against those who would destroy his version of the only true democracy.

Henry Clay was almost the antithesis of Calhoun. Correctly described by enemies as the "victor of many a well-fought bottle," admittedly an almost compulsive gambler at cards, and with an attractiveness for women which inspired much gossip, Clay was widely loved by a public which would never elect him President. A slaveholder who considered slavery evil, Clay was a leader in the African colonization movement. Knowing his own weaknesses, Clay easily forgave the sins of others. His role as the Great Pacificator in the sectional quarrel was well-earned.

Like Calhoun, Clay detested Andrew Jackson, but unlike Calhoun, Clay kept his views clear and consistent. He spent a lifetime working for an America in which a strong and paternalistic central government would promote economic growth through protective tariffs, a national bank, an adequate paper money system, and federal financing of roads, canals, river and harbor channels, and other such internal improvements. He hoped that slavery would some day disappear but prayed that any attempted solution of the issue would be delayed as long as possible.

The Death of Slavery

Daniel Webster of Massachusetts shared Clay's economic views both on principle and from personal interest. He was a heavy investor in factories and a highly paid attorney for the Bank of the United States. Magnificent in appearance and with a superb voice and command of words, Webster was established by the mid-1830's as the great orator of nationalism. He had been a states' rights adovcate at the Hartford Convention of 1815, and had opposed the tariff and the Bank in 1816 and 1817. As New England turned to manufacturing, however, Webster by 1828 was answering brilliantly all his own earlier arguments. As Southerners opposed the tariff in the name of states' rights, Webster found nationalism a powerful emotional instrument for use in rebuttal. In phrases unmatched before or since, except possibly by Lincoln's Gettysburg Address, Webster held aloft a vision of the great and indissoluble American Union which set fire to men's hearts everywhere. Like many men, Webster was captivated by his own arguments and became totally dedicated to a role perhaps begun originally on a note of sophistry. Fate played cruel tricks on Daniel Webster. For the presidency he was always a step behind Clay as a candidate because Clay had wider popular support. In 1840 and 1848, however, Webster haughtily refused nominations for Vice-President. These were the only two elections won by his party in its history, and in each case the President was soon stricken with a fatal illness.

Just as dedicated to the Union as Webster and Clay was their lifelong opponent, Thomas Hart Benton of Missouri. Benton was a strange blend of Southern agrarian economics and western vision. In one breath he would astound listeners with predictions of a future continental America of 160,000,000 people bound together by steam cars racing at 100 miles an hour across the prairies and plains, and in the next he would insist upon the abolition of all paper money except large bills. Even before Webster and Lincoln he was preaching the concept of the United States as a great universal experiment in democracy destined to change the course of human events throughout the world.

Although Benton had exchanged shots with Andrew Jackson, by the 1830's the two had long since been reconciled and Benton had become a worshiper at the Jackson shrine. He was the acknowledged senatorial spokesman and administration leader for both Jackson and Van Buren.

From a combination of personal and political considerations and genuine conviction, Benton in 1832 began denouncing Calhoun as an enemy of the Union. He saw first the tariff issue and then the slavery question as problems which the Carolinian was deliberately exaggerating and distorting for the sake of political ambitions. Like Clay and Webster, Benton hoped and believed that time, economic disadvantage, and perhaps the hand of Providence would eventually enable the United States to eliminate slavery without bloodshed. He was certain also that the racial difference was the only serious obstacle to an ultimately peaceful solution. Benton condemned the abolitionists as foolish incendiaries who were in reality hurting the cause they were promoting, but he reserved his bitterest attacks for those Southerners like Calhoun who in his opinion were playing directly into the hands of the abolitionists.

In his speeches over a thirty-year period and in his two-volume *Thirty Years View*, completed in 1856, Benton offered in advance the first of the modern revisionist views of the coming of the Civil War. The abolitionists and the Southern fire-eaters, he wrote, were the two blades of a pair of scissors.

The Death of Slavery

Alone neither could harm the Union; together, if unchecked, they would cut it in half. Benton's view of his own "blundering generation" differed occasionally in the selection of the "blunderers" from that of James Randall some ninety years later, but the general thesis was the same. Similarly, the exaggerations and distortions described by Avery Craven and Allan Nevins in the 1940's were nowhere discussed with greater contemporary understanding than in the words of Benton.

Benton's views were shared by his friend, Francis Preston Blair, editor of the Jacksonian newspaper, the *Globe*. "The Nullifiers," wrote Blair in 1835, "are far more numerous and talented than the Abolitionists. They give a striking proof of their superior adroitness, in the use they make of their rivals in the evil work of disunion." As Jackson's personal editor and chief dispenser of administration ideas and principles to some four hundred other Democratic papers, Blair was a powerful force in the Jackson and Van Buren administrations. Blair dramatized in stirring language the philosophy of Jacksonian democracy and contributed directly to much of the nation's reforming spirit. Until the 1850's, however, he sharply opposed the abolitionists, and saw no inconsistency in this opposition.

The ancient patriarchs and bitter enemies, Andrew Jackson and John Quincy Adams, remained influential well into the 1840's. The indomitable Jackson returned to his Hermitage plantation near Nashville, Tennessee. Still possessed of great popular appeal, the old man kept his place in the hearts of disciples on the political stage. A benevolent slaveholder, Jackson abhorred the abolitionists, but he was never able to take them very seriously as a genuine threat to the South.

Elected President in 1824, Adams was magnificently equipped for the position in every respect but two. He possessed knowledge, ability, dedication, and vision, but he did not project a warm or colorful image, and he was unwilling to be a politician. He refused to fire his enemies, hire his friends, or use his powerful office in any way to win loyal supporters and workers. His dreams, plans, and programs were systematically frustrated by Congress, and he suffered a humiliating defeat at the hands of the backwoods general, Andrew Jackson, in 1828.

By the late 1830's, Adams, still somewhat bitter and cynical but as independent-minded as ever, was back in Washington as a representative. He was an abolitionist primarily because he recognized the unhappy impact of the institution on the nation as a whole, and the petitions against slavery in the District of Columbia won his immediate support. With Theodore Dwight Weld as an adviser, Adams year in and year out defended the right of the petitioners to have their plea heard. His speeches won him the sobriquet Old Man Eloquent from supporters, but many less complimentary titles from others. In defending the right of petition on principle, Adams at one point sought unsuccessfully to introduce a petition from certain citizens calling for a breakup of the American Union. His purpose was clear to the sophisticated observer, but appeared little short of treason in the Democratic presses. The right of petition was a holy principle for many Americans, however, and the alliance of Adams and the abolitionists for its defense greatly increased the respectability of abolitionism in many northern communities.

Martin Van Buren, Jackson's heir apparent, was elected President in 1836. His career, wrote William Cullen Bryant, had been "one of unobtrusive usefulness, not of turbulent injury." "Little Van" was loved by fierce partisans like Jackson, Benton, and Blair, but he was very different from them in personality.

The Death of Slavery

He was a man of sophistication and humility who lacked his friends' capacity to reduce political issues to struggles between light and darkness. He found the role of a warrior politician an impossible pose, and no amount of *Globe* rhetoric could make him a second Jackson.

Extensive wildcat banking and a flood of banknotes supported by their acceptability as payment for public lands had brought a great boom in land sales and business expansion. Fearing the rising inflation and unable to persuade Congress to check the bubble, Jackson in 1836 had the Treasury issue a "specie circular," requiring hard money for public lands. Overnight millions of dollars in banknotes became worthless and many local banks collapsed. Meanwhile, the banks in which Jackson had placed the national treasury had loaned out much of it before the deposit bill of Calhoun and Clay required them to transfer the federal funds to the states. This ruined many of these banks, and two successive years of American crop failures and a tightening of credit in Europe completed the picture. The prosperous America which had elected Van Buren became overnight an unhappy land of unemployment, bankruptcies, business failures, and foreclosures.

Jackson had ruled a Democratic party badly divided, but held together by Old Hickory's power at the ballot box and the advantages of membership in a victorious party. Van Buren had no such magic, and the depression left him open to attack from every direction.

Van Buren blamed the national banking system which had caused the inflationary boom in the first place. He was compelled to issue treasury notes to keep the government afloat, but his permanent solution was the creation of a new independent treasury which would keep and disburse government funds, and be entirely unconnected with either banking or paper money. The program finally passed Congress in 1840, but not before it had caused angry divisions in the Democratic party.

The small group who had been closest to Andrew Jackson—men like Van Buren, Blair, Benton, Polk, Taney, and Wright—were democrats in political philosophy, but conservative on economic questions. In ringing phrases they called for greater equality of opportunity for all Americans to share in the nation's wealth and power. Simultaneously, except for Indian removal and cheap land, they opposed banking, tariff, currency, and internal improvements programs designed to enlist the federal government in the movement to create more total wealth for Americans to share. Men who had risen to great power by preaching democracy found their most cherished economic principles threatened by the very hopes and ambitions they had done so much to stimulate. Even in the days of Jackson, significant numbers of nominal Democrats had supported Whig policies, and Old Hickory's most important victories had come through his use of the veto. Democrats had overwhelmingly supported the deposit act whereas only a handful had favored Jackson's specie circular.

In 1840 the Whigs took full advantage of the recent though fading depression, divisions among the Democrats, and the unspectacular image of President Van Buren. They nominated William Henry Harrison, the ancient hero of Tippecanoe. They adopted no platform and forbade Harrison to utter a word on any issue. In a series of speeches and pamphlets they produced a devastating collection of falsehoods about Van Buren. The President was pictured as a "sweet sandy-whiskered," overfed eastern aristocrat, who pranced about in corsets, spent much time before the mirror, wasted immense sums of public money on personal luxuries, and ate nothing but gourmet delicacies off golden plates. Even the installation of a bathtub in the White House became a major crime. Harrison in contrast was a rough-and-ready hero who had fought Indians and the British and was possessed of all the homely virtues of the frontier and the farm. Harrison was the candidate who would be content with a log cabin, plenty of hard cider, and an occasional cold shower or dip in the creek. In vain did the Democrats point out that only one wing of the Harrison mansion had any logs in it and challenge the candidate to take a stand on significant issues.

Harrison's Whig followers included both abolitionists and slaveholders, but the latter were at least partially mollified by the selection of John Tyler of Virginia as the vice-presidential running mate. Democrats tried to make an issue of Harrison's onetime membership in an abolition society, but the Whigs countered with a more recent event. An obscure naval officer was convicted of extreme cruelty on the evidence of a large number of white sailors and three Negroes. When Van Buren accepted the verdict of the court-martial, which had also been approved by all subordinate authorities, the Whigs flooded the South with pamphlets accusing the President of accepting Negro testimony against a white officer.

In the end Harrison was elected, and American politicians had learned some new lessons in the art of gaining votes. The new President, however, already ailing in body and spirit, found the constant badgering and pleading of his followers for political appointments almost unendurable. From a variety of causes, including the job itself, Harrison died only a month after taking office.

With Whig majorities in Congress, leaders like Clay and

Webster returned to Washington determined to undo all the wicked works of Andrew Jackson and get America again on the road to their "American system." They were not prepared, however, for John Tyler. Finding himself unexpectedly in the White House, Tyler promptly reverted to the principles of a states' rights Virginia planter. The Whigs voted the independent treasury out of existence and twice passed laws chartering a new national bank. Each time President Tyler vetoed this central policy of his adopted party. The tariff likewise met the same fate until a destitute treasury compelled him to accept a set of moderate duties in 1842. The Whigs passed Clay's program for distributing the proceeds of federal land sales to the states for internal improvements, but even this was eliminated by a rider declaring it void if tariffs should rise above 20 per cent. By 1843 Clay had resigned from the Senate, all of Tyler's cabinet except Webster had resigned, and the Whig party was in chaos, its splendid victory of 1840 turned to ashes by the obstinacy of John Tyler.

As the Whigs continued to thrash about in their own web, the Democratic presidential nomination for 1844 glittered ever more brightly. With no Jackson or any other dominant personality in sight, the stage was set for America's first real intraparty fight for a party nomination. The raucous, gamelike election of 1840 had avoided the significant problems. That of 1844 would create issues destined to plague Americans for a generation.

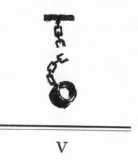

V

"If the Union Is to Break..."

In 1844 personal ambitions and bitter rivalries of long standing, a major national issue, and a Presidential election combined to generate new sectional quarrels and link them irrevocably with America's inevitable march to the Pacific.

Although Henry Clay was the only obvious Whig candidate for President, the Democratic party of 1843 had a surplus of would-be men of destiny.

Martin Van Buren, clearly a victim of inexcusable chicanery in 1840, hoped for vindication. Indeed, the renomination of Van Buren in 1844 had become an obsession with ideological Jacksonians like Blair, Benton, and Silas Wright. The ability of ordinary people to vote intelligently was an essential part of the Jacksonian faith, but in 1840 Americans had responded to the crudest emotional appeals and had elected Harrison with no knowledge of his principles. To the Jacksonians this was a blow against democracy itself, and American voters had to be given a chance to vindicate themselves by electing Van Buren in 1844.

Northwesterners disenchanted with Jacksonian economic policies were far less enthusiastic about another effort for Van Buren. Governor Cass of Michigan was available, as was James Buchanan of Pennsylvania. Former Vice-President Richard M. Johnson also stood ready for the call. Johnson had supposedly slain the Indian chief Tecumseh at the Battle of the Thames in 1813, and this achievement plus a reputation for sympathy with industrial workers had brought him to the political heights despite an unorthodox personal life which included illegitimate daughters by his mulatto housekeeper.

Many Southern Democrats still dreamed of seeing Calhoun in the White House, and the Carolinian, having regained his Democratic status in the service of Van Buren, was still hopeful. Other nominal Democrats, having received recent favors from the President, were even advancing the claims of John Tyler because of his vetoes of key Whig policies. By the end of 1843 numerous public meetings, public letters, and editorials were expounding the virtues of each candidate.

Van Buren's opponents won their first victory by getting the convention scheduled for May, 1844, instead of the preceding fall or winter. Otherwise Van Buren would have been nominated. Although the little New Yorker lacked the Jackson aura of invincibility, many Democratic officeholders owed their jobs to him, and his prestige as an ex-President remained strong among local party workers. In state convention after state convention resolutions were passed pledging the delegations to his support.

Discouraged but not ready to surrender, the friends of both Tyler and Calhoun, meanwhile, found an issue whereby to dramatize their candidates. Texas had been a prominent question for seven years. In 1843 it suddenly became an overwhelming problem.

Texas had been settled by American frontiersmen attracted by the promise of 640 acres at twelve and one-half cents an acre. The Mexican government had invited them, allowed them to bring slavery despite Mexican laws against it, and given them full citizenship.

The political instability of Mexico and the differences in background and outlook, however, brought almost immediate trouble. The Texans were tough, acquisitive, energetic, and aggressive both with each other and with others. The Mexicans enjoyed afternoon siestas and did not feel that fortunes and empires had to be built every day. To the Texans the Mexicans appeared lazy, shiftless, and untrustworthy. Many Mexicans felt that the Yankees rushed through life so fast that they ran by more than they caught. There were also specific grievances. In 1830 Mexico passed laws forbidding further emigration to Texas and abolishing slavery. The Texans protested unsuccessfully in petitions and memorials, and Stephen Austin spent eight months in prison after delivering the resolutions of a Texas convention. By 1835 the revolution was in full swing. Americans were horrified to learn of the massacres at the Alamo and at Goliad, and there was widespread rejoicing in the United States when General Sam Houston defeated Santa Anna at San Jacinto in 1836 and thereby liberated Texas.

In Washington the United States Senate debated long and hard before recognizing the new Republic of Texas. Abolitionists protested that the affair was a slave plot to extend the wicked institution, and Benjamin Lundy published a pamphlet which required little reading beyond the title page: *The War*

"If the Union Is to Break . . ."

in Texas: A Review of Facts and Circumstances Showing That This Contest Is a Result of a Long and Premeditated Crusade against the Government Set on Foot by Slave Holders, and Perpetuating the System of Slavery and Slave Trade in the Republic of Mexico. In the Senate various moderates assailed the Lundy position and defended the Texans. "It may as well be said that our revolution was a war for the extension of slavery," said Thomas Hart Benton. "No revolt, not even our own, ever had a more just and a more sacred origin." Calhoun, however, insisted that the abolitionists were in fact correct. Texas, he said, should not only be recognized, but should be immediately annexed openly for the purpose of preserving and extending slavery. The North, insisted Calhoun, had a duty to annex Texas as a show of good faith and goodwill toward the South. The senate voted to recognize, but not to annex.

In 1837 President Van Buren declined a Texas petition for annexation on the ground that this would mean annexing a war with Mexico. In 1842 Tyler took the same position because of the opposition of Secretary of State Daniel Webster. Most Americans, leaders and people alike, apparently looked upon Texas as a fruit still green, but to be easily plucked as soon as it ripened. The American trade with Mexico was extensive and valuable, and there appeared to be no reason for a costly and perhaps bloody premature consummation of the inevitable union.

In the background, meanwhile, certain forces were working as a catalyst. Texas had issued more than $7,500,000 worth of bonds, which by 1841 had passed largely into the hands of well-placed Americans who had bought them for much less than their original value. Simultaneously, Texas had issued land warrants for many millions of acres, and many of these were soon acquired by American speculators waiting for the rise. Money for propaganda urging the annexation of Texas was not difficult to obtain.

In 1843 the impatient President Houston began to combine feigned indifference toward the United States with well-publicized friendly personal relations with the British chargé d'affaires, Captain Charles Elliott. Elliott had just been recalled from Canton for losing a battle of wits to a Chinese viceroy. The Chinese had destroyed some twenty thousand chests of illegal British opium, a mistake for which the *Times* pronounced Elliott "notoriously unfit to manage a respectable apple stall." Anxious to retrieve his reputation, Elliott suggested a plan for Britain to provide Texas with a large loan and free trade in exchange for the abolition of Texas slavery.

Various British editors had already discussed the commercial advantages to British cotton and sugar colonies if Texas and, indeed, the entire American South should abandon slavery, and Elliott's proposal received widespread publicity. Apparently, however, the only official British act was an unaccepted recommendation to Mexico that she offer recognition in return for emancipation. Though admitting that abolition in Texas would be desirable, the British foreign secretary, Lord Aberdeen, assured both the Texas envoy and United States minister Edward Everett that Britain planned no interference with Texas. He had proposed a loan, said Lord Aberdeen, but his colleagues had refused to agree; the subject of slavery had not even been discussed in connection with the request.

In contrast, Calhoun's confidant and former editor, Duff Green, who was in England lobbying against the corn laws, reported that England had in fact offered a loan in exchange for emancipation. Calhoun and his friends chose to believe Green.

"If the Union Is to Break . . ."

So did the patriarch of Nashville, Andrew Jackson, who was still withstanding both his illnesses and the atrocious treatments of his doctors. Senator Robert J. Walker, who was involved in both land scrip and bonds, wrote Jackson a letter which drew upon the old man's hatred of all things British as a skilled violinist draws his bow. With equal skill Sam Houston assured his old commander that Texas had twice gone to the altar in a wedding dress. If abandoned a third time, the bride would seek another bridegroom. Houston had done enough courting to know the power of jealousy. Jackson responded with a long letter urging the immediate annexation of Texas.

Southern fears for Texas were paralleled by a growing northwestern appetite for all the Oregon Territory up to 54° 40', which was the southern boundary of Alaska. In 1818 the United States and Britain had agreed to a joint occupation, and in 1827 this had been renewed with a stipulation that either could end the agreement on a year's notice. By 1844 Americans had settled in the Columbia River area and had a reasonably clear title by right of occupation to the area now comprising Washington and Oregon. The British, meanwhile, had also settled on the Columbia, as well as along the Fraser River to the north. It was clear that Britain would not lightly surrender access to the Pacific, but for some northwesterners this was no argument. They would have "Fifty-four forty or fight!"

Anxious to get northwestern support for Texas, Robert J. Walker gave leaders from that section reason to hope that a grateful South would be happy to oppose Britain in the Far North as well as in Texas. Walker also made a remarkable emotional appeal to the Northwest in a public letter. Slavery, said Walker, was declining and would soon disappear in Missouri, Kentucky, and northern Virginia, and the states immediately northward might well be inundated by a mass migration

The Death of Slavery

of free Negroes. Texas, however, would open a gateway to the southward and provide an outlet for slaves and slavery to move not only into Mexico and Central America, but perhaps entirely off the North American continent. The letter shrewdly appealed to both racists and those anxious to spread America westward without the economic blight of slavery. Numerous Americans looking ahead to the future free states of Iowa, Kansas, Nebraska, Minnesota, and the Dakotas could take comfort from Walker's "safety valve" argument.

As Texas and Oregon came to dominate the press, the forgotten man in the White House, John Tyler, began to dream of annexing Texas himself and thereby winning reelection over his enemies in both parties. John C. Calhoun, meanwhile, again tasted the bitterness of disappointment as the narrowness of his Southern base of support daily became more apparent.

In 1843, Daniel Webster resigned as Secretary of State and was replaced by Calhoun's friend, Abel Upshur. Encouraged by the President, Upshur ignored the assurances of Minister Everett and assumed without question that the British were moving against slavery in Texas. Upshur offered Sam Houston a treaty of annexation and a promise of military protection against Mexico.

The path to statehood for Texas thus appeared to be wide open, but one stumbling block remained. The Texas constitution of 1836, in keeping with the later Texas reputation for thinking in big terms, had defined the boundaries of the new Lone Star Republic to include large parts of four other Mexican states, including almost two-thirds of present-day New Mexico. Since the Upshur treaty did not mention boundaries, Texans and Mexicans alike could only assume that the United States was preparing to support the Texas claims by force.

"If the Union Is to Break . . ."

Upshur's role suddenly came to a tragic end. On February 28, 1844, a happy bipartisan group of government leaders and their wives and friends boarded the USS *Princeton* for a Sunday cruise down the Potomac. A special attraction was the firing of a new rifled naval gun called the Peacemaker. In the morning the passengers marveled at the noise, smoke, and accurate trajectory. During a final exhibition enroute home in the afternoon, the Peacemaker exploded, killing six persons, including Upshur, Secretary of the Navy Gilmer, and David Gardiner. (Gardiner's beautiful twenty-three year old daughter had rejected an offer of marriage from the widower President. The tragedy changed the young lady's outlook, and President Tyler soon gained a bride.)

Because of Tyler's peculiar status with both parties, outstanding candidates for the vacant posts were scarce. Like Tyler, however, John C. Calhoun had also done some traveling between the parties, and he was available. Tyler reluctantly offered Calhoun the Department of State, and Calhoun "reluctantly" accepted.

The new Secretary promptly sent a military and naval force south to protect Texas, and on April 12, 1844, he signed the treaty begun by Upshur. Unless accompanied by conciliatory offers to Mexico, the treaty carried to its logical conclusion could mean only a war with Mexico or an abject surrender by Mexico of a vast area never part of the Mexican state of Texas. Land-hungry Americans both north and south, however, might still have supported the treaty but for Calhoun's next move.

Having signed a treaty which to be ratified would need all possible bipartisan and national support, Calhoun turned the question into a bitter sectional argument and an instrument for wrecking Van Buren's presidential nomination. After the *Globe*

67

announced that Van Buren and his friends would whole
heartedly support the "reannexation" of Texas, Calhoun de
layed the announcement of the treaty for another week an
executed a maneuver calculated among other things to chang
Van Buren's mind.

Just before his death Secretary Upshur had received a
official letter from the British government emphatically deny
ing any plans against Texas slavery or against the interests o
any other Southern state. The letter, however, ended on
moralistic note: "Although we shall not desist from those ope
and honest efforts which we have constantly made for pro
curing the abolition of slavery throughout the world, we sha
neither openly nor secretly resort to any measures which ca
tend to disturb [the Southern states'] internal tranquillity."

To this brief statement Calhoun published a long answe
which condemned the British for threatening slavery in Texas
and the United States, announced his treaty of annexation, and
concluded with a detailed eulogy of slavery as a wise and
humane institution. Thus no Northerner could vote for the
treaty without voting thereby for the moral righteousness of
slavery. If Northerners would not do this, wrote Calhoun to a
friend, it could only mean "that the spirit of faction and opposition to the South on the ground of slavery are stronger
than the love of country."

Calhoun described his British correspondence as an opportunity to force the slave issue which he intended to exploit to
the fullest, and whether Texas itself or the opportunity for a
showdown on slavery was his primary objective is impossible
to determine. As early as December, 1843, the *Madisonian*, a
Tyler-Calhoun paper in Washington, had stated that the defense
of slavery required either secession or the incorporation of

Texas, and this theme continued throughout the spring and summer of 1844. Representative Lewis of Alabama assured Calhoun that if the treaty were rejected he would "consider the Union at an end." Francis Pickens felt the South "bound in self respect and self preservation to join Texas with or without the Union." Governor Hammond of South Carolina added: "If the Union is to break there could not be a better pretext. With Texas the slave states would form a territory large enough for a *first rate power.* . . . The North and the South cannot exist united." Hammond insisted that "four-fifths of the South prefer Texas to the Union and are prepared to stand by that issue if made." In all these letters to Calhoun the writers clearly expected a sympathetic response.

On April 27, 1844, the leading contender of each party published a letter on the question of Texas. As expected, Henry Clay opposed immediate annexation. To the dismay of his ancient mentor, Andrew Jackson, Van Buren took a similar position. The Little Magician traced the history of Texas for six columns to show that Texas was legally part of the United States and should be and would be annexed, but he insisted further that the step should be preceded by termination of the war between Texas and Mexico and a settlement of the existing boundary disputes with Mexico. Two days later Jackson's other protégé, Benton, took the same ground and expressed the further heresy that the boundaries being claimed by Texas were unjustifiable. The *Globe* shocked Jackson further by praising Van Buren and Benton, although it stressed those parts of their letters which called for the peaceful and honorable annexation of Texas whenever this should become possible.

Old Hickory agonized over the Van Buren and Benton letters, concluded that Benton as the stronger must have been responsible, and found but slight comfort in a speculation that the *Princeton* explosion, which had knocked Benton unconscious, might have permanently damaged his old friend's brain. The old man fired a letter to the press reemphasizing his personal affection for Van Buren and explaining that the New Yorker had not been fully informed of the British threat and would surely change his position now that he understood the facts. It was an attempt to give Van Buren a second chance, but from New York came only silence.

Their all-out support for immediate annexation would have insured the Democratic nomination for Van Buren, kept Blair in his lucrative position as party editor, and left Benton's Missouri enemies impotent in a state hot for Texas. All three loved Andrew Jackson dearly and suffered from his displeasure. They were also professional politicians in the business of courting popular favor. For years, however, they had glorified their leader, Jackson, as an incorruptible and immovable hero who always did right regardless of the personal cost or danger, and they had been captured by the image they had created. Van Buren was obviously influenced by public opposition to the treaty in New York, and the other two men were affected by loyalty to Van Buren. All three, however, believed they were risking disaster entirely for principle, and their fury against Calhoun knew no bounds.

In the Senate Benton denounced the treaty as a threat of spoliation and robbery against Mexico, an attempt to promote disunion, and a bomb designed to blow up presidential hopefuls in favor of "a new Texas candidate, anointed with gunpowder." On June 8, 1844, the treaty was defeated by a 35-to-16 vote, with only eleven of the twenty voting Southerners supporting it.

"If the Union Is to Break . . ."

Calhoun described his mixed motives and double disappointment in a letter:

had hoped to draw out a full correspondence by my letters to Mr. ackenham . . . and I Doubt not, what was intended would have een accomplished, had the Senate done its duty and ratified the reaty. Their neglect to do so, I fear, will not only lose Texas to he Union, but also defeat my aim in reference to the correspondence. . . . It will, I fear, be difficult to get another so favorable to ring out our cause so fully and favorably before the world. I shall mit none, which may afford a decent pretext for renewing the orrespondence.

Benton's final apostasy came after he introduced a bill to annex Texas with certain conditions: a carefully defined boundary eaving the Rio Grande valley to Mexico; assent of Mexico to e obtained by treaty or omitted according to the will of Congress; and the creation of a single state of Texas as large as the argest existing state and the division of the remaining territory qually into slaveholding and non-slaveholding areas. This program, said Benton, would bring Texas into the Union without n unjust war with Mexico and without a sectional struggle which could cause a civil war. The bill lost by a small margin. n the debate Senator McDuffie of South Carolina warned that Calhoun's slain treaty, like Caesar's ghost at Phillipi, would aunt Benton in the forthcoming Missouri election. Perhaps so, nswered Benton, but with one difference. Rather than take his wn life as Brutus did, he would save himself "for another day, nd for another use—for the day when the battle of the disnion of these States is to be fought—not with words, but with ron—and for the hearts of the traitors who appear in arms gainst their country." The words brought applause from the allery and a handshake from an ancient enemy, John Quincy Adams. "Mr. Adams," said Benton, "you are passing off the stage, and I am passing away also, but while we live, we will stand by THE UNION."

News of a Benton-Adams handshake was almost more than Andrew Jackson could bear. "Do my dear Mr. Blair inform me if this can be true," the old man pleaded. "If it is, I want no better proof of his derangement."

Even before the treaty's defeat, the Democrats had met in convention at Baltimore on May 27. The telegraph was still a new toy, and anxious groups of people in Washington waited for reports on the newly strung wires between Washington and Baltimore. A combination of southern and western delegates engineered by Robert J. Walker established a two-thirds rule for the voting. Van Buren began with a considerable majority, but could not get the required two-thirds. The spirit of Andrew Jackson was present in favor of Texas immediately and all of Oregon, and ultimately the convention settled on Jackson's view that his fellow Tennesseean "Col. Poke" would be a good candidate. It was James K. Polk and a resolution that "our title to the whole of . . . Oregon is clear and unquestionable. . . . the reoccupation of Oregon and the reannexation of Texas, at the earliest practicable period, are great American measures, which this convention recommends to the cordial support of the democracy of the Union." Van Buren's New York friend, Senator Silas Wright, rejected the nomination for Vice-President, and the ex-President's only consolation prize was a resolution assuring him of "the deeply-seated confidence, affection, and respect of the American democracy." The convention closed on a high note. In his farewell speech, Chairman Wright of Pennsylvania was moved "to weep at the thought that this monument of mind before me must pass away, in the change of all things! . . . It will last, and be fresh on the pages of our country's history, when the pyramids of the Nile shall have crumbled, stone by stone, to atoms."

At the *Globe* Blair struggled to remain loyal to Van Buren and Benton, intercede for them with Jackson, and support the Polk candidacy. He and his partner John Rives also bet $22,000 on the election of Polk, a fact which pained his conscience every time he wrote an editorial against Clay's excessive gambling. Tyler's friends also nominated the President as an independent candidate. The *Globe* enjoyed attacking both Tyler and Clay until Tyler withdrew, and orders came from Jackson to support Polk and "let Tiler alone."

The election of 1844 was far from a popular mandate for Texas, and perhaps proved little more than Henry Clay's confirmed status as an unlucky politician. In New York the abolitionists, who were unsatisfied with Clay's view that at some future date under more favorable circumstances Texas might enter the Union as a slave state, supported the Liberty party. Their candidate, James Birney, received almost 16,000 votes in New York, which Clay lost by only 5,000 votes. Had Clay won New York he would have been elected President by seven electoral votes. Nationally, the combined popular vote for Clay and Birney exceeded Polk's popular vote by some 24,000, but Polk had a substantial electoral margin.

When Congress met in December, 1844, the annexationists moved the simple admission of Texas to the Union by a majority action of each house. After a debate of almost three months, Walker won over the five Senate votes led by Benton by offering an amendment which gave the President a choice between the conciliatory Benton approach and the Calhoun program. Assuming that Polk would make the decision and assured by Jackson and others that Polk would stand on the Louisiana

The Death of Slavery

Purchase of 1803 in determining boundaries, the Benton forces capitulated. The joint resolution passed the Senate by a scant two votes. It also authorized Texas to divide itself into five states and extended the Missouri Compromise line on slavery. The first proposal, which would have given the South eight extra senators, was never seriously considered. The latter one was rendered meaningless by geography.

When the joint resolution was passed, the Tyler administration had three days left in office. Almost immediately an envoy was dispatched to Mexico with an unqualified and unconditional offer of annexation already approved by Congress. Boundaries were not mentioned.

The annexation of Texas had divided the Democratic party, opened the way to war and future territorial expansion, and irrevocably joined the process with a fierce sectional quarrel over slavery. It had become a manufactured political instrument as well as a national project, and in some ways an excuse for sectional discord as much as a reason. Whether or not any or all of this was necessary or inevitable was now purely academic. A train of events had been set in motion, and the end was nowhere in sight.

VI

For the Fulfillment of Our "Manifest Destiny"

Resolved: That the present war with Mexico . . . is now waged ingloriously,—by a powerful nation against a weak neighbor,—unnecessarily and without just cause, at immense cost of treasure and life, from which slavery has already been excluded, with the triple object of extending slavery, of strengthening the "Slave Power," and of obtaining the control of the Free States, under the Constitution of the United States.

LEGISLATURE OF MASSACHUSETTS

The annexation of Texas was entirely justifiable because that region had already won its independence. The additional territory taken from Mexico, however, was a different matter. The "manifest destiny" of the United States to become a continental nation and the weakness of the Mexican government's hold on

The Death of Slavery

the vast lands from New Mexico to the Pacific have satisfied the consciences of most modern Americans. It is true that Mexico ruled this area with frightful inefficiency and occasional oppression, and that the United States has since used it more wisely for the benefit of more people. The unique Mexican brand of slavery, Indian peonage, disappeared under American influence, the Mexican inhabitants kept their property and became citizens of the United States, and economic opportunities for the humbler members of society were probably increased by the transition. There is also reason to believe that California's substantial American minority, like the Texans, might have separated the area from Mexico without outside interference and thereby made it a natural candidate for peaceful annexation to the Union. Indeed, the peaceful surrender of New Mexico and the very minor resistance of California indicate a strong possibility that both might have been taken without a war if the United States had conceded the Mexican title to the territory between Texas and Mexico actually in dispute. Ironically, the war may have been caused in part by the feeling of American leaders that seizure of California would be dishonorable unless accompanied by a war for which the blame could be cast upon Mexico. None of this, however, alters the fact that the war began with a Mexican attack upon an American army which had advanced some 140 miles into territory that had never been in law or in fact anything but Mexican. In the end the only Mexican failing that counted was military weakness.

In 1819 the United States had relinquished all title to any of Texas in a treaty with Spain. The Mexican revolution had achieved independence from Spain for all of Mexico, including the Mexican province of Texas. The Texas boundaries established by Mexico could be changed by negotiation or by

76

conquest, but not by a simple decree of the leaders of the new Texas. Had the Texans been able to take and hold any of the disputed territory by themselves, the United States claim would have been stronger, but the Texans could not claim the disputed areas by right of either conquest or occupation. Indeed, by 1843 the Texans had twice been repulsed in efforts to seize Santa Fe, New Mexico.

The Mexican War handed the United States a vast and fabulously rich area for a relatively small cost in blood and treasure. Ultimately, however, the price was compounded many times. Except for the existence of slavery itself, no single situation or event contributed so much to the coming of the Civil War as did the War with Mexico.

In 1845 the American presidency was not quite the isolated, Olympian pinnacle it has since become, and the responsibilities appeared less awesome in their magnitude. No President had yet been assassinated, although a young psychopath had contributed to the Jacksonian legend of invincibility by trying unsuccessfully to shoot President Jackson from a distance of less than a yard. The caps fired, but the charges failed to explode in his two pistols. The Presidents continued to go unguarded, and a presidential interview at the White House was a relatively easy matter for almost any ordinary citizen. Indeed, the harrassments of job-seekers were a major hazard of the office. For long periods of time no crises appeared, and the nation seemed capable of at least reasonable progress whether its leadership was strong, weak, wise, or atrocious. Numerous American Presidents left no personal mark on their nation at all. Occasionally, however, the character of the man in the White House was very important indeed.

"Who is James K. Polk?" sneered the Whigs in the campaign of 1844. The election results answered the question partially, and Polk came to Washington determined to dispel any lingering doubts as to his identity.

The mother of James Knox Polk was the great-grandniece of John Knox, the founder of Scotch Presbyterianism, and her son was equipped with a stubbornness, devotion to duty, and independence worthy of this ancestor. Proud, sensitive to slights both real and imagined, and always certain of the purity of his own motives, Polk, like his mentor Jackson, rarely took a tolerant view of his opponents. His wife, Sarah Childress Polk, was beautiful, childless, and puritanical, and as first lady she kept White House social life at a minimum. Their apparently quiet and serene life together left Polk almost full time for introspection and concentration upon his duty and his career.

After a highly successful period as a Tennessee lawyer and planter, Polk served President Jackson well as a leader in the House of Representatives. After fourteen years in the House and a term of much power and influence as Speaker, Polk in 1839 surrendered a relatively secure seat to run for governor of Tennessee. It was an unselfish attempt to save Tennessee from what he considered the evil clutches of Whiggery, and Polk succeeded, but for only one term. He was defeated for reelection as governor in both 1841 and 1843, and he always believed that his sacrifice and his efforts had gone unappreciated. His plea for a new administration press in Tennessee had gone unanswered, and he had felt neglected by the official Democratic *Globe*.

By late 1843 Polk had his heart set on vindication by a vice-presidential nomination, and he was resentful when the *Globe* presented the claims of W. R. King of Alabama as well as his own. The nomination for the top spot was a heady surprise, but his victory was as much a challenge as a triumph. Too many Democrats regarded Polk as an accidental President of limited capacity, and hoped to make his administration a vehicle for their own ambitions. Aware of this almost to the point of obsession, the new President was prepared to take orders only from the Almighty and then only according to his own interpretation of the divine commandments.

Polk had many virtues and capacities, but the ability to reunite the Democratic party was not one of them. In the days of Jackson, Polk had fought side by side with Martin Van Buren, and his lingering respect and loyalty toward the leader he had supplanted was genuine. After exchanging several friendly letters with Van Buren, Polk offered the Treasury and War Department cabinet posts to the New Yorker's devoted friends Silas Wright and Benjamin F. Butler. Van Buren thought New York should have the State Department, but obviously this post could not go to anyone "soft" on Texas. Wright had already refused the nomination as Polk's vice-presidential running mate, and had since agreed to run for governor of New York. His rejection of the Treasury Department was polite but firm. Butler wrote Polk that he was willing to be Secretary of State or of the Treasury, but that the War Department would not be worth the personal sacrifices it would require. Two days later Butler received an unfortuitously delayed letter from Van Buren urging him to accept the War Department, and Van Buren's son, Smith, was speedily rushed off to Washington to assure Polk that Butler would reconsider, but it was too late. Polk was irritated by such temperamental irresolution, and various southerners and westerners had been working hard to convince him that the Van Burenites did not really matter anyhow. Smith Van Buren arrived to find that the War Department had gone to his father's New York enemy, William Marcy, and that Robert J. Walker was to be Secretary of the Treasury. The Van Burens immediately concluded that Polk had made insincere offers which he knew would be rejected, but most of the fault was clearly theirs. In a note to Martin Van Buren, Mrs. Butler took full blame for her husband's decision. The lady may have cast a long shadow. Had her husband become Secretary of War certain important events of the next four years might have come out quite differently.

Friends had already warned Blair that his *Globe* spoke too much for one faction of the party and had urged him to take a new partner more receptive to other viewpoints. Jackson's nephew, Andrew J. Donelson, was recommended, but Blair and Rives disliked Donelson for financial as well as political reasons. They had already lost money endorsing his notes. They would stand by their principles and take what came. Polk's personal feelings against Blair ran deep. He had been told the unlikely story that after his 1843 defeat in Tennessee Blair had said that Polk would be remembered by the Democratic party only when he redeemed his own state. Most important, the *Globe* was still loyal to Van Buren and Benton, and Polk, correctly enough, would share authority and prestige with no one. From the Hermitage Jackson urged the President to keep Blair and the *Globe*, but "Col. Poke" was his own man. He dismissed Blair as administration editor, and Blair, co-operatively enough, sold his paper to Thomas Ritchie of Richmond for $100,000. Blair could now develop his new Silver Spring plantation and build Jackson Hall (one story for rented stores and a restaurant, the upper floor for the Democratic party) with the $22,000 won on Polk's election. The dismissal was a personal humiliation, however, and caused much anger in Blair's wide circle of friends. Polk offered Blair the mission to

Spain, but the angry John Rives objected so strongly that he offered to pay Blair's ambassadorial salary if he would refuse. Rives' offer was not taken seriously, but his objections won out over the feeling of Blair's wife and daughter that a sojourn in Spain would be pleasant.

John C. Calhoun rejoiced in his enemies' apparent fall from influence, and hoped for a time that he might remain in the cabinet. On Jackson's advice, however, Polk offered Calhoun the mission to England, "there to combat with Lord Aberdeen the abolition question." Calhoun refused, and his friends were soon complaining that the local offices everywhere were going to "Benton, Blair, and the New York regency."

Worrying but little about the hurt feelings or disappointments of ambitious colleagues, the President outlined a herculean program and proceeded to work himself to death for its accomplishment. He would complete the Texas settlement for the maximum advantage of the United States. He would try to fulfill his campaign pledge on Oregon. He would take California because that Mexican province was unstable as Texas had been, and rumors had placed a British fleet in a threatening position. This Pacific prize, along with Oregon, was coveted by American commercial interests dreaming of a rich oriental trade, as well as by would-be settlers ready to start the covered wagons moving toward their final stopping place on the Pacific. A thoroughgoing Jacksonian agrarian, Polk would also push for a lower tariff and a renewal of Van Buren's independent treasury. James K. Polk was essentially a man of peace who loved the American Union and opposed anything and anyone who would sow discord among the sections. His most cherished goals, however, proved unattainable without war and the sharpest divisions within his party and the nation.

Few Presidents have ever asked or received less assistance

from a Secretary of State in reaching major decisions than did
Polk. Secretary of State James Buchanan vacillated constantly,
and the few strong positions he took were usually ignored by
his chief.

With the annexation of Texas, Mexico had broken relations
with the United States. Polk was willing to pay up to $40,000,-
000 for New Mexico and California, but a channel of communications had to be reopened first. Unhappily, Polk's first
unofficial envoy, William Parrott, held a much exaggerated
financial claim against the Mexican government, and his arrival
in Mexico City touched off a wave of popular anger which
made the mere recognition of his presence impossible for any
Mexican official or aspiring politician. Parrott was followed by
John Slidell, whose status as "envoy extraordinary and minister
plenipotentiary" made the United States itself the object of any
insults he might receive. When the Mexican government flatly
refused to discuss anything with Slidell except the Texas
boundary, General Taylor was ordered to the mouth of the
Rio Grande River. In part for recognizing Slidell at all, the
Mexican government was overthrown on January 4, 1846, by
a military regime pledged to resist every Yankee demand. In
March Slidell gave up and returned home.

Slidell believed that the Mexican stubbornness was encouraged by a belief that the United States would have serious
trouble with Britain over Oregon. Polk, however, was certain
that if the United States lowered its tariffs on British manu-
factures and the British abolished their corn laws against American grains, the Oregon boundary would be no problem. Encouraged by the unanimous views of his cabinet, he pushed the
Mexican quarrel to a showdown. Citing the insults to Slidell
and the Mexican refusal to pay claims due American citizens,

For the Fulfillment of Our "Manifest Destiny"

Polk prepared a request for war. On Saturday, May 9, however, word came that General Taylor's army had been attacked north of the Rio Grande. The event occurred some 140 miles south of the border of the former Mexican state of Texas, but just north of the boundary set by the Texas Republic. On Sunday the President rewrote his request: Mexico had "shed American blood upon American soil." In his diary he also confessed a deep regret over having been compelled to work on Sunday. Within three days the Congress with but few dissents passed a declaration of war. John C. Calhoun blamed the entire business on Polk, and he and three followers refused to vote. Numerous others soon regretted their too easy capitulation to the excitement of the moment.

With one war underway, Polk also "looked John Bull in the eye" over Oregon. The President offered a compromise at the forty-ninth parallel. The British demanded the Columbia river valley. Polk advanced to a bold demand for 50°40′. The British receded to 49°. Reluctant to stand alone in violating his platform pledge for 54°40′, Polk asked the Senate for advice on the treaty before signing it. After a three-day speech by Thomas Hart Benton documenting fully the historical correctness of 49°, the exhausted Senate voted for its acceptance and on June 15 ratified the treaty by 41 to 14. The opposition was short on numbers, but long on noise. Northwesterners with sons and friends risking death in Mexico demanded "Fifty-four forty or fight!" but the only fighting was against Mexico for lands far to the South. Secretary Buchanan objected to Polk's sharp notes to the British on the ground that war might result, but later refused to draft Polk's message communicating the proposed treaty to Congress because it settled for less than 54°40′.

Northwesterners soon felt betrayed by the South again. With

The Death of Slavery

the Senate margin only one vote, Congress passed the Walker tariff, which raised duties on luxuries and lowered those on necessities. Northwesterners helped the South pass the bill, but northwestern wool-growers felt sorely neglected. Also by a small margin Congress passed a new independent treasury system, and again northwesterners joined with an overwhelming Southern vote. Meanwhile, in a vote which appeared to be part of a bargaining process, Congress also passed a bill for extensive federal improvements on northwestern harbors, rivers, and lakes. The chief opposition came from the Southern friends of Calhoun. Receiving the rivers and harbors bill first, Polk kept it unsigned until delivery of the tariff and independent treasury bills. Then he vetoed the rivers and harbors bill on constitutional grounds. Some historians have called the bill a pork barrel measure, but northwesterners already angry over Oregon saw it differently. Chicagoans named the forbidding sandbar at the mouth of the Chicago river "Mount Polk," and charged the President and the slavocracy with indifference to their lives and property. Democratic and Whig papers alike took up the cry against the Slave Power, which was endangering the lives of sailors and stifling the progress of Northern cities, towns, and farms. After Texas was annexed, the Ohio abolitionist Joshua Giddings had announced that the "Union formed by our venerated predecessors" had been replaced by "a new slave-holding confederacy, with a foreign government." This was a gross exaggeration, but in 1847 it began to make sense to men who felt they had a God-given natural right to such blessings as protected markets, lighthouses, unencumbered harbors, snag-free rivers, and all of Oregon.

Northwestern bitterness against the South was more than matched by the fury of northeasterners who considered the war an unholy and wicked crusade in the cause of slavery. Indeed, the blood shed in Mexico was like oil thrown upon the fires of a sectional conflict hitherto only smoldering. *"Resolved,"* said the Massachusetts legislature by an overwwhelming vote:

That such a war of conquest, so hateful in its objects, so wanton, unjust, and unconstitutional in its origin and character, must be regarded as a war against freedom, against humanity, against justice, against the Union, against the Constitution, and against the *Free States;* and that a regard for the true interests, and the highest honor of the country, not less than the impulses of Christian duty, should arouse all good citizens to join in efforts to arrest this gigantic crime, by withholding supplies, or other voluntary contributions, for its further prosecution, by calling for the withdrawal of our army . . . aiding the country to retreat from the disgraceful position of aggression which it now occupies towards a weak, distracted neighbor and sister republic.

"If I were a Mexican," declaimed Thomas Corwin of Ohio on the Senate floor, "I would tell you, 'Have you not room in your own country to bury your dead men? If you come into mine, we will greet you with bloody hands and welcome you to hospitable graves.' " Praise for Senator Corwin rang throughout the North. As the war dragged on, Henry Clay and Daniel Webster, both of whom had opposed the policies which had produced the war, each received the somber word that a son had fallen. Public sympathy for the famous parents added further to the opposition to the war and the anger against the Slave Power.

Representative David Wilmot of Pennsylvania became the instrument of an inevitable Northern response with his proviso outlawing slavery in any new territories to be taken from Mexico. The proviso was an amendment to a bill providing money for negotiations with Mexico, and it became part of every appropriations debate for the next two years. In 1846 and 1847 it passed the House but was defeated in the Senate.

In February, 1847, Calhoun answered with a series of resolutions questioning the constitutionality of the Missouri Compromise and insisting that in all territories all states must have equal rights, including the protection of slavery. Otherwise, Calhoun grimly warned, "Political revolution, anarchy, civil war, and widespread disaster" would result. Benton charged Calhoun with "introducing needless firebrands to set the world on fire," while others from farther north were certain the Carolinian was plotting to steal the great Far West for slavery. Calhoun and his followers steadfastly opposed all appropriations for finishing the war and brought the slavery question into every debate. Regarding the slavery argument as dangerous foolishness for the mere sake of political ambition, the slaveholding President was soon denouncing Calhoun as "the most mischievous man in the senate to my administration."

As he grew thinner, paler, and ever more determined, Polk continued to suspect his fellow Democrats of putting 1848 ambitions ahead of 1846 and 1847 duties, and he struggled on with the war. The command of the armed forces is the one responsibility that most American Presidents have been least prepared for, and Polk was no exception. All in all, however, his correct judgments outweighed his mistakes, and he was in some respects uncommonly lucky.

Antonio Lopez de Santa Anna had successfully deceived the Spanish, the Mexican revolutionaries, the Church, and a long succession of both friends and enemies, and James K. Polk in 1846 was, therefore, the victim of both talent and experience. Soon after the war began, an envoy from the exiled Santa Anna in Cuba came to Polk with an offer to end the war on favorable terms for the United States in exchange for safe transportation back to Mexico. An American gunboat picked up Santa Anna, took him through the naval blockade, and landed him at Vera Cruz. With his usual sense of honor, the *caudillo* almost literally landed shouting denunciations of the United States, and he was soon appointed commander of the Mexican armies.

Santa Anna, however, was not a military genius, and his territory was infinitely vaster than his legions were numerous. Soon Thomas Hart Benton brought his old friend James Magoffin, a wily American trader from Santa Fe, for a long conference with President Polk. Magoffin returned to New Mexico, and when the American army under General Kearny arrived in New Mexico a few months later, the Mexican generals surrendered without a shot. The Mexican generals acquired unexplained affluence, and Congress later voted Magoffin $30,000 for undescribed services to his country.

Meanwhile, a joint effort from the sea under Commodore Stockton and overland by a small force under Captain John C. Frémont had easily conquered the vast and rich province of California. Unhappily for Frémont, General Kearny arrived soon afterward and assumed the governorship which Commodore Stockton had already conferred upon Frémont. Frémont was a remarkable blend of courage, energy, stubbornness, and stupidity. He was also the son-in-law of Senator Benton, and he had successfully defied superior authority once before when his eighteen-year-old bride destroyed some unwelcome orders and sent her supposedly unsuspecting husband off to explore the West with an expedition already ordered disbanded by the Secretary of War. Since he enjoyed being governor, Frémont chose to obey the navy, and when word from Washington finally vindicated Kearny, the Pathfinder found himself under arrest and facing court-martial on various counts of mutiny and disobedience. None of this, however, interfered with the rapid and complete annexation of California by the United States.

These rich and easy conquests seemed to win the President but few friends outside the South, and the Whigs won both houses in the Congressional election of 1846. With most of Polk's objectives won, the problem of forcing Mexico to admit defeat and make peace remained.

The two leading major generals, Winfield Scott and Zachary Taylor, were reportedly Whigs, and Polk's personal relations with them became such that even intelligent communications were difficult. Polk's entire cabinet considered Taylor "unfit for command," and Scott had been something of a Democratic political problem since the days when President Jackson had relieved him of command during the ill-fated war with the Florida Seminoles. "Gen'l Taylor's feelings," Polk confided to his diary, "are anything but friendly to the executive Government. . . . He has no sympathies for the administration and cares only for himself." Taylor in fact did not favor territorial expansion and wished only for the war to end. The President considered Scott "not only hostile, but recklessly vindictive" toward himself and his administration. Scott was addicted to writing public letters, which the President usually considered treasonable at worst and "highly unjust and disrespectful" at best.

For many months Polk's chief military adviser was Thomas Hart Benton. The Missouri senator supported the administration's domestic programs and led the debates over military appropriations. He also presented Polk a military plan for an invasion at Vera Cruz and a march upon Mexico City, to be coordinated with a separate invasion from the north. In response

For the Fulfillment of Our "Manifest Destiny"

to Polk's complaints about the disloyalty of his generals, Benton suggested the appointment of a chief with the rank of lieutenant general and with authority to plan overall strategy and negotiate for peace at the auspicious moment. The assignment, said Benton, would require statesmanship and wisdom as well as bravery, and if necessary he would take the job himself. The new rank, however, would require an act of Congress.

Various historians have derided Polk's attempt to create this post for Benton, but few contemporaries questioned Benton's competence. He had served as a colonel in the War of 1812, and as a longtime chairman of the Senate Committee on Military Affairs he knew both the personnel and the weapons of the armed forces. He was also well-versed in military history and strategy, had a thorough knowledge of Mexican geography, history, and politics, spoke fluent Spanish, and had numerous Mexican contacts. The plan failed because Whigs and Calhoun Democrats feared it would make Benton the next President, and because expansionist Democrats led by Walker, who wanted to annex all of Mexico, feared Benton would negotiate an excessively generous peace treaty.

Congress refused to create the new office, but after Polk had appointed Benton a major general, the House of Representatives voted to authorize the President to appoint his own commander-in-chief, regardless of seniority. By a small margin, the Senate refused to concur. Polk wanted Benton to go to Mexico as a major general, but Benton would go only as commander-in-chief with authority to make peace. The cabinet, led by Secretary of War Marcy, insisted that under existing law a junior major general could not be given command over his seniors. Polk was willing to recall both Scott and Taylor, but could think of no reason for recalling Generals Butler and

The Death of Slavery

Patterson. Learning, however, that Butler was either ill or wounded in New Orleans, Polk urged Benton to wait for the possibility that General Patterson might also be eliminated. "I did not still see my way entirely clear to remove three senior Major-Generals who had rank of Gen'l Butler," the President wrote, "but thought it possible that I might do so in a short time." Benton, however, was not inclined to go to the front as the single replacement for four experienced major generals. It was the only sane decision, but the harrassed, overworked President considered it a shirking of duty. Relations between the President and the Senator were never again the same.

A few weeks later, Frémont arrived in Washington to stand trial for insubordination in California. Benton represented his son-in-law in a spectacular court-martial which ended in Frémont's conviction and dismissal from the army and, incidentally, made the young officer a national martyr. In review, Polk accepted Secretary Marcy's recommendation. He approved the findings, but remanded the sentence and ordered Frémont restored to full rank. Frémont and Benton, however, considered the trial a vendetta by West Pointers against an officer who had risen from the ranks. To them the approval of the findings was a mortal insult. Frémont resigned from the army, and his father-in-law never spoke to Polk again. Benton remained a loyal Democrat, but his alienation from Polk weakened the appeal of their party for many who still considered the Missourian the personification of Jacksonian Democracy. Frémont, who deserved most of his troubles, became a heroic symbol for Polk's enemies in both parties, and was destined to become the first presidential candidate of the new Republican party in 1856.

The war finally ended on a bizarre note. An earlier plan to

send a distinguished bipartisan peace commission was dropped because of opposition to Polk's insistence that John Slidell must be included. Secretary of State Buchanan did not want the peacemaking assignment, but he was also reluctant to give the opportunity to any future rivals in his own party. Neither he nor the President wished to send a possible presidential contender, even though it was their last chance to gain some credit for their party to offset the fame acquired by Generals Taylor and Scott. In the end, State Department clerk Nicholas Trist, husband of Thomas Jefferson's granddaughter and ex-secretary to Andrew Jackson, was dispatched to Mexico. As long as Trist quarreled with Scott over their overlapping authority, Polk considered his envoy incomparable. When, however, a gift of wine and jelly from Scott cured a stomach pain for Trist and a friendship developed, the President abruptly changed his mind. When Trist, like so many before him, was deceived by Santa Anna and granted a premature armistice which the wily Mexican immediately violated, Polk discharged Trist and ordered him home. Trist, however, in an action perhaps uniquely American, ignored his President's orders and eight weeks later signed a peace treaty. For $15,000,000 and the assumption of $3,250,000 worth of claims against Mexico the United States received New Mexico, Arizona, Utah, California, and Texas as defined by Texas. Polk was furious at Trist, but the unemployed civilian had driven a bargain no government could reject. The Senate ratified the treaty, but Trist received neither salary nor reimbursement for his expenses until 1871.

On February 21, 1848, while the Senate was debating Trist's handiwork, the eighty-year old John Quincy Adams collapsed at his desk in the House. Anxious friends carried him to the

Speakers' office, where he lay struggling for life for more than forty-eight hours. A peaceful death finally came, however, and Old Man Eloquent lay stilled at last. Amid the eulogies by friends and foes alike, John C. Calhoun was conspicuously silent.

During the next twelve months President Polk watched his party ignore the ambitious cabinet members Walker and Buchanan and nominate a presidential candidate without asking his advice. Thanks in part to Secretary of War Marcy, who used the patronage of his office to strengthen the conservative New York Democrats, the liberal New York Democrats split off to form the Free Soil party. As a result, when the weary Polk left the White House for the last time in March, 1849, Zachary Taylor, the Whig general Polk disliked most, was waiting to move in. None of this made the retiring President very happy, but he returned to Tennessee firm in the conviction that he had served his nation well. Three months later he was dead. After many decades of neglect, history has concluded that his problems were indeed exceedingly difficult, his achievements impressive, and his failures not caused by any lack of devotion or dedicated effort for his country.

By the end of the Mexican War, the slavery question had a new dimension. Few Americans had thought seriously about tampering with slavery in states where it already existed. Its introduction into new areas, however, was a different matter. By keeping slavery out of the new territories, northeasterners could ease their consciences over a war considered wicked and unjust from the beginning, and in their region the awareness of slavery as a moral evil was most acute. Northwesterners, less worried about international morality and the inhumanity of slavery but still smarting over Oregon, Polk's vetoes, and parts of the tariff, could fervently join a crusade to thwart the wicked and all-powerful slavocracy and keep the West a region of free land and free men.

To Southerners, meanwhile, the right to take slavery into new territories, even where geography and climate forbade it, took on a new symbolic value in the face of the Wilmot Proviso and the increased volume of the attacks upon their section. Calhoun's constant warnings had penetrated the surface of Southern feelings and stirred up their normal competitive instincts. People who feel they are sitting on a lighted bomb need reassurances, and perhaps the loud Southern demands for unusable rights in the territories were merely attempts to check the length of the fuse.

In 1848 Oregon received a territorial government with an antislave restriction, and the Whigs once again elected a general to be President of the United States. Oregon brought the slavery argument again to a blaze. The election created the Free Soil party and thereby became another important milestone on the road to civil war.

VII

Retreat from the Abyss

We . . . owe a great example to a struggling and
agonized world. . . . They see us almost in a state
of disorganization—legislation paralyzed—distant
territories left without government—insult violence outrage on the floors of Congress. . . . our an-
cestors . . . left us the admiration of the friends
of freedom throughout the world. And are we to
spoil this rich inheritance—mar this noble work—
discredit this great example—and throw the weight
of the republic against the friends of freedom
throughout the world?

THOMAS HART BENTON, 1849

There was peace with Mexico but a new conflict in Washington.
In far-off Oregon the settlers had outlawed slavery, and by
the spring of 1848 two Oregon delegates were begging Congress
for the blessings of a territorial government. Abolitionist John
Hale of New Hampshire introduced an amendment barring
slavery, and Calhoun replied that this meant "the degradation

of nearly one-half the States of this Union, who claim to be full equals here, and who intend never to yield that full equality." Come to Mississippi, said Senator Henry Foote to Hale, and we will hang you to our tallest tree. Be our guest in New Hampshire, replied Hale, and you will receive the respect due a senator. Hale withdrew his amendment, but the Southerners were equally adamant against the antislavery constitution proposed by the Oregonians.

Moderates pointed out that slavery was impossible in Oregon, and pleaded with both sides to stop the meaningless quarrel. "We read in Holy Writ," said Thomas Hart Benton:

that a certain people were cursed by the plague of frogs. . . . You could not look upon the table but there were frogs, you could not sit down at the banquet but there were frogs, you could not go to the bridal couch and lift the sheets but there were frogs! We can see nothing, touch nothing, have no measures proposed, without having this pestilence thrust before us.

The summer was long and hot, and tempers ran high. No one thought slavery could go to Oregon, and everyone agreed that with statehood Oregon could settle slavery in its own way. The principle of Southern rights in a territory, however, was debated as a life-and-death matter. In July a bipartisan committee proposed a compromise. Oregon should be organized with its antislave laws, and California and New Mexico should be organized with a provision against any action on slavery by their territorial legislatures. It was argued that any actual case involving slavery in California or New Mexico would be decided by the courts. If, as people expected, no slaves went there, the controversy would end. The Senate passed this compromise after an exhausting twenty-one hour debate. Before the weary members had recovered, however, the House had tabled their bill. After more weeks of bitter argument, the Senate in another all-night marathon voted to extend the Missouri Compromise line to the Pacific. Again the House disapproved. On the last day of the session the Senate debated until 9:00 A.M. Sunday morning amid fierce tensions and before crowded galleries. In the end, the two slaveholders Benton and Sam Houston joined with the North, and by the scant margin of their two votes, Oregon received a territorial government which barred slavery.

"The great strife between the North and the South is ended," said Calhoun. The bill would "convert all the Southern population into slaves. . . . The separation of the North and the South is completed. . . . This is not a question of territorial government, but a question involving the continuance of the Union."

The buckskin-clad Houston answered that slave restriction in a territory north of forty-two degrees could not possibly harm the South. He was "of the South, and he was ready to defend the South; but he was for the Union. The Union was his guiding star, and he would fix his eyes on that star to direct his course. . . . He would discourage every attempt to sow discord, and to stir up the passions of the country, and kindle them up to war."

The Oregon debates coincided with the early stages of the presidential campaign. The Democrats tried to neutralize the slavery issue and regain the Northwest by nominating Lewis Cass of Michigan. Cass had argued strongly that the people in each territory should decide the question of slavery for themselves. Cass had a record of achievement as a frontier leader and governor for eighteen years of the huge Michigan Territory (modern Michigan, Wisconsin, Iowa, and Minnesota). By 1848, however, he was sixty-six, fat, colorless, and uninspiring.

Retreat from the Abyss

Having won only one national election in their history, the Whigs sought to duplicate this feat by again nominating a candidate—Zachary Taylor—who could run as a military hero totally uncommitted on important issues. Jefferson Davis, whose first wife was General Taylor's daughter, momentarily encouraged the Democrats to consider Old Rough-and-Ready one of their own. Taylor, however, who had never voted, was persuaded otherwise by Thurlow Weed and William H. Seward, and perhaps by some of his quarrels with President Polk. The antislavery delegations from New England and Ohio opposed the slaveholding Taylor, but the Whig convention voted down a resolution affirming the power of Congress to control slavery in the territories, and in the end Taylor was nominated. Once again with a victory in sight, the great Whig statesman, Henry Clay, had been pushed aside by those for whom victory was more important than the principles or abilities of their candidate. No candidate of intelligence and proved ability—even one as moderate as Henry Clay—could fail to encounter opposition on the slavery question. The totally inexperienced and semiliterate military hero, on the other hand, had popular appeal, and could be marketed to the voters as a split personality on the slave issue. Taylor's campaign was managed by the antislavery New Yorker, William H. Seward, but it was vague enough to win the votes of most Southerners. Seward had no apparent difficulty reconciling his antislavery reputation with Taylor's ownership of more than a hundred slaves. It was a sad commentary on the state of American politics, and it was the beginning of the death rattle for the Whig party.

Almost equally important, when the Democrats convened, two delegations appeared from New York. In a typical Democratic effort at harmony, the convention voted to seat both and give each delegate half a vote, but the liberal Barnburner faction withdrew in anger. They soon met at Utica, New York, and nominated Martin Van Buren for President. Seven weeks later the Barnburners reconvened at Buffalo in company with other antislavery Democrats, Liberty party men, and "conscience" Whigs to form the Free Soil party. In a shouting, singing, roaring convention that resembled a religious revival, they renominated Van Buren with Charles Francis Adams as his running mate. Van Buren had engineered Jackson's first victory over Adams' father, John Quincy Adams, and had been a lifelong political enemy of the Adams family, but the union was entirely harmonious. Their slogan: "Free soil, free speech, free labor, and free men!" Their platform: "Opposition to the aggressions of the slave power," support for antislavery territorial governments, and demands for a tariff, a frugal government, river and harbor improvements, and free homesteads for actual settlers. The platform was appealing, and the party had quality—men like William Cullen Bryant, Francis P. Blair, Preston King, Samuel J. Tilden, Charles Sumner, C. C. Cambreling, and Salmon P. Chase. The major parties had the presses, the patronage, and the ties of past loyalty, however, and to most voters outside the Northeast the Free-Soilers appeared far more radical than they actually were. Van Buren and Adams received only 10 per cent of the total vote, but it was enough to defeat Lewis Cass. In New York, Van Buren outran Cass 120,510 to 114,318, and the New York electoral vote would have elected Cass. The Free Soil party fared remarkably well in the Northeast, and its leaders would comprise a Republican nucleus eight years later. Once again the Whigs had elected a President.

In 1850 the sectional quarrel reached a climax in a memorable session of Congress. The elder giants, Clay, Webster, Calhoun, and Benton, made their final Senate appearances and gave histrionic performances which have become monuments to their careers. Younger men like Seward and Jefferson Davis, however, spoke in new accents that would shape the future. The democratic process of debate, compromise, and acceptance of compromise was stretched almost, but not quite, to the breaking point. Compromises were finally possible in 1850 because there were concrete issues which provided the basis for give and take, and because in 1850 the extremists in Congress did not really speak for a majority of their constituents. The crisis developed naturally enough. In January, 1849, Calhoun renewed his attack with an "Address to the Southern Delegates in Congress," which warned that Northern opposition to slavery in the territories was only a step toward abolition and a bloody race war. The "Address" caused no great stir in Congress but received wide publicity in the Southern press. In October, 1849, Mississippi issued a call for the Southern states to meet in convention at Nashville on June 1, 1850, and the secessionists were clearly hoping that the impending quarrels would prove irreconcilable.

In January, 1848, the peace and serenity of Johann Sutter's great and beautiful California ranch were destroyed forever when an employee found gold near Sutter's Fort. Overnight some 100,000 immigrants scrambling for riches poured into California by land and sea, and every kind of lawlessness quickly followed. Amid the thievery, claim-jumping, violence, murder, and open vice, the desperate need for law and order was clear.

California had too many people and too many problems for territorial status. In September, 1849, a convention wrote a state constitution, and the people soon elected state officials and a delegation to Congress. A majority of the Californians were of Southern origin, and the first governor, lieutenant governor, and United States senators were Southerners, but the constitution forbade the introduction of slavery. When Congress met in December, 1849, California stood begging for admission to the Union. Since the United States was losing millions in gold from government land, and since California met every qualification for statehood, the admission should have been routine, but to various Southern leaders the antislave provision was a mortal insult. To Southern radicals, states' rights was a sacred principle for slaveholding states, but it was obviously not a blessing to be wasted on people who opposed slavery. One of the new California senators, incidentally, was John C. Frémont, who had returned to California to find gold and reach one of the high points of his up-and-down career.

Meanwhile, Texas was again in the limelight. The Texas constitution of 1836 had defined all of New Mexico east of the Rio Grande (two-thirds of the present state and the only part then with white inhabitants) as part of Texas. Twice during the brief period of the Lone Star Republic, Texans had invaded New Mexico. The first expedition of three hundred men had been imprisoned for several years, and a second force of two hundred men sent to intercept traders had been captured and disarmed by a United States military escort. The Texans considered their title a solemn obligation of the United States. When New Mexico surrendered to General Kearny, however, its people were promised that New Mexico would keep its traditional boundaries. The Federal government thus found itself with conflicting commitments.

Only the parties involved should have been concerned, but Texas was a slave state whereas New Mexico was a free territory. Slave state leaders quickly took the side of Texas, and practically everyone else felt sympathy for New Mexico.

Retreat from the Abyss

In March, 1848, Texas designated the disputed area Santa Fe County and appointed a judge for the district. Santa Fe papers recommended that the newly appointed judge bring soldiers to protect him from tar and feathers, and the stalemate continued. In September, 1849, New Mexico wrote a territorial constitution which ignored slavery, although slavery there had long been illegal, and the appointed congressional delegate stressed the impossibility of slavery in a well-publicized letter to Daniel Webster. In December, 1849, Texas subdivided the previous Santa Fe County into four smaller, equally theoretical counties and declared a showdown. The legislature called for mobilization, and public meetings all over the state demanded military action if necessary.

President Taylor, who had a fierce personal dislike for Texas, was determined to protect New Mexico. An agent was dispatched to New Mexico with promises of protection and instructions to the New Mexicans to stand firm and work for statehood. The appearance, at least, of a slow but steady collision course between a United States army and a Texas force supported by other Southern states was in the background of all congressional debates on the subject in 1850. On June 13, Henry S. Foote warned the Senate that one shot against Texas would bring every "heroic son of the South" and probably "hundreds of thousands of gallant and true-hearted men in the North" to the rescue. The result would be "Rivers of blood and scenes of butchery . . . more shocking than ever yet stained the pages of history." On July 3, President Taylor threatened to lead the United States army against Texas personally, and warned the unionist Whigs, Toombs and Stephens of Georgia, that if they rebelled he would hang them.

The long-standing demand for abolition in the District of

Columbia, meanwhile, had been watered down to a far more popular movement for abolition of the slave trade in the District. The anomaly of the clanking chains, human pens, and shouting noises of slave auctions within earshot of the Capitol of a nation that claimed to be the freest on earth was obvious, but many Southerners still feared the action as a possible opening wedge to some future catastrophe. Less powerful, but also frightening to Southerners, was a budding movement against the entire domestic slave trade, and this proposal was especially obnoxious in states of the upper South which were steadily sending more and more of their slaves southward.

The major practical grievance of the South in 1850 was the loss of slaves who escaped to the North and could not be recovered because of the Underground Railroad, occasional help to the fugitives from individual northerners, a lack of police assistance in some states, and direct legal barriers in others. The actual number of escapees was greatly exaggerated, but this problem, like that of antislavery restrictions in far northern territories, had a symbolic significance. If Northerners were honest in their protestations that no attack on slavery in Southern states was intended, let them prove their goodwill by passing a federal statute to help Southerners regain their escaped property.

The Congress of 1850 began with a quarrel over the right of Father Matthew, a well-known Irish priest imported to preach temperance to New England working people, to be a guest on the Senate floor. Some twenty years earlier the good churchman had written an article criticizing slavery, and this was enough to deny him the privilege after two days of bitter argument. For seven weeks, sectional acrimony and useless quarreling prevailed, although there was time for a hot strictly party debate on a motion to sever relations with Austria because of the suppression of the Hungarian revolution. Ritchie's *Daily Union* dubbed the Whigs the Austrian Party, and roasted them for subservience to European tyranny.

Because of the Speaker's importance in selecting committees, the House remained without a parliamentary leader after sixty ballots and various threats of physical violence on the floor itself. The Free-Soilers held the balance of power and sought to make deals exchanging their support in the organizational process for assistance in their drive to bar slavery in the territories. Not until December 23 was Howell Cobb of Georgia chosen.

In January, 1850, Henry Clay was almost seventy-three. Thirty years earlier Clay had steered the Missouri Compromise through Congress, and he was now prepared to leave the stage on an equally high note. Enlisting the support of Daniel Webster, who even in this final moment acted again in the shadow of Clay, he offered his compromise: admit California with no congressional action on slavery, which meant a free California; authorize territorial governments for New Mexico and Utah without mention of slavery; assume the Texas debt in return for Texas' relinquishing part of its claims against New Mexico; abolish the slave trade in the District of Columbia, but pass a resolution that slavery itself should remain there as long as it existed in Maryland or until Maryland and the District should accept compensation for a voluntary emancipation; give the South its fugitive slave law; and recognize the principle that Congress had no jurisdiction over the domestic slave trade.

Clay's resolutions provided a basis for concrete debate, and the halls of Congress soon rang with proffered amendments and roaring speeches. It was clear that very few were for all of the propositions, but that a majority for each was entirely probable. Four groups quickly developed: Northerners against any compromise; Southerners against any compromise; those professing support but insisting that all the propositions be passed in one bill; and those supporters who argued that each measure must be voted on separately.

On March 4, the dying Calhoun, wrapped to the chin in flannels, tottered to his Senate seat and informed a hushed crowd that a colleague would read his speech. Like Clay, the Carolinian remained in character to the end. The Southern states, said Calhoun, feared they could no longer remain in the Union with honor and safety, because soon there would be forty Northern senators against only twenty-four from the South. This in turn would mean the inevitable destruction of everything the South held dear. This inequality, insisted Calhoun, was due entirely to three types of government legislation: measures like the Northwest Ordinance of 1787, the Missouri Compromise, and the recent Oregon bill, all of which had denied Northern territory to Southerners; economic policies which had caused wealth to flow from South to North and thereby prevented immigration to the South; and, finally, those laws and precedents which had changed the federal republic into a consolidated democracy. No compromise, said Calhoun, could protect the South or save the Union. The North could save the Union only by conceding the South an equal right in the territories, enforcing the fugitive slave laws, ceasing all abolition agitation, and providing a constitutional amendment which would guarantee the South the power to protect itself. California was the test question, and the alternatives were plain. If the North would not agree to these requests, said Calhoun, "say so; and let the States we both represent agree to separate and part in peace. If you are unwill-

ing we should part in peace, tell us so, and we shall know what
to do, when you reduce the question to submission or
resistance."

With all its tragic overtones and dramatic power, Calhoun's
dying message was as inconsistent as the career it attempted
to justify. Calhoun had spent years promoting the sectional
discord he now deplored, and the threats and injustices he cited
were grossly exaggerated. The Northeast and the Northwest
were not united against the South on any question except that
of extending slavery, and the South had more than held its own
on most issues, including the recent acquisition of Texas.
Common agrarian interests would keep the Northwest and
South together on most economic questions, unless they should
be divided by other factors. Calhoun declared that antislave
restrictions barred all Southerners and implied that without the
legal barriers the Old Northwest, Iowa, and Oregon would
have become slave areas. Actually, many hundreds of thousands
of Southerners had moved into the regions cited just to escape
the slave system. Calhoun blamed the tariff for the lack of
Southern immigration, but the duties had actually gone steadily
downward since 1833. Slavery itself was the great deterrent
against foreign and northern immigration to the South. Calhoun's charge that America had become a consolidated democracy in which the non-slaveholding states had a numerical
superiority was correct. His corollary prediction that this would
eventually compel the South either to secede or endure a forced
abolition of slavery has achieved a certain faint validity in
the ideological atmosphere and events of a century later, but
it was not justified by the existing realities of 1850. In 1850
Congress had a long and consistent record of non-interference
with Southern slavery. Constitutional abolition would have

required an amendment which even in the later Union of fifty states the former slave states could block. There was no indication that the representatives of the most property-conscious people on earth would ever enact an unconstitutional law destroying Southern slave property and then vote the arms and men necessary to carry it out. Calhoun's final view that the South might secede in peace or successfully fight for independence would be tested later.

Three days after Calhoun's last speech, Daniel Webster rose for his final great oration. His role had been cast in the immortal "Reply to Hayne" in 1830, and he was still in character, but with a new tolerance and magnanimity toward the same foes. "I wish to speak today," said the godlike Daniel, "not as a Massachusetts man, nor as a Northern man, but as an American." The extremists on both sides, he said, were mistaken. Right could not be separated from wrong with mathematical precision, and the issues must be solved through mutual charity, concession, and compromise. In language almost arrogant in its self-confidence, Webster agreed with Calhoun that the American future lay with the free states, but he pleaded with his fellow Northerners to accept victory graciously and avoid insult to the South. The Wilmot Proviso, he said, was clearly unnecessary in California and New Mexico, and he would abandon it as a needless indignity to the South: "I would not take pains uselessly to affirm an ordinance of Nature, nor to reenact the will of God."

Having proffered the olive branch, Webster turned his guns full blast against the secessionists, including Calhoun, "who, I deeply regret, is prevented by serious illness from being in his seat today."

Retreat from the Abyss

"The Senator from South Carolina is in his seat," said a sepulchral voice.

Webster smiled and spoke directly to Calhoun: "Peaceable secession is an utter impossibility." Referring to the coming Southern convention at Nashville, Webster ridiculed the very thought of "hatching secession over Andrew Jackson's bones."

Webster sat down amid wild applause, but Calhoun was on his feet. "I cannot agree," he quavered, "that this Union cannot be dissolved. Am I to understand . . . that no degree of oppression, no outrage, no broken faith, can produce the destruction of this Union? . . . the Union *can* be broken." Webster answered that the Union could indeed be broken, but that such an event would be a revolution. Calhoun rose and tottered through the Senate door for the last time.

A few weeks later Calhoun died alone, leaving his last tortured effort on a few scraps of paper. The Constitution, he wrote, should be amended to provide two Presidents, one from each section, and no law should become effective unless signed by both. Calhoun's death brought a momentary pause in the general rancor, and his Washington funeral was magnificent. Clay, Webster, and other veterans rose to pronounce brilliant eulogies, but Benton was as silent as Calhoun had been after the death of Adams.

Webster, meanwhile, was denounced throughout New England for compromising with Satan. His constituents could accept the law of God against slavery in the territories, but his support for the fugitive slave law was another matter. "I know no deed in American history," said Theodore Parker to a great meeting in Boston, "done by a son of New England to which I can compare this but the act of Benedict Arnold." "Of all we loved and honored," wrote John Greenleaf Whittier in the poem *Ichabod*,

> ... naught
> Save power remains:
> A fallen angel's pride of thought,
> Still strong in chains.
>
> All else is gone; from those great eyes
> The soul has fled;
> When faith is lost, when honor dies,
> The man is dead!

Henry Clay, despite failing health, was never more eloquent in his appeals for reason and patriotism. Individual man, he said, was but "a mere speck upon the surface of the immense universe —not a second in time, compared to . . . eternity. . . . Let us look at our country and our cause; elevate ourselves to the dignity of pure and disinterested patriots, wise and enlightened statesmen, and save our country from all impending dangers. What if, in the march of this nation to greatness and power, we should be buried beneath the wheels that propel it forward. What are we—what is any man worth who is not ready and willing to sacrifice himself for the benefit of his country when it is necessary?"

Calhoun was dead, but younger Southerners echoed his demands and looked to the future. To Jefferson Davis, Clay's program was no compromise at all because it gave the South nothing. Davis demanded the extension of the Missouri Compromise line all the way to the Pacific Ocean, with the South to have full rights to take slaves to any territory, including California, south of the line. Even this would be a Southern concession, he said, and anything less would be an intolerable aggression. If the South, said Davis, "was to be debarred from

cquiring by emigration, by enterprise, by adventure, by toil,
nd labor—equally with others, from the common domain of
he Union," the Union would soon reach the condition pre-
licted by Calhoun, "when, without an amendment of the
:onstitution, the rights of the minority will be held at the
nercy of the majority." Davis offered no specific amendment,
out insisted that one was necessary to protect the South. Any
lenial of slave rights in the territories would "give additional
oower to a majority to commit further aggressions upon the
ninority," and to this he would never consent. Like Calhoun,
Davis felt that all agitations against slavery must cease. Slavery,
ne said, required no apology. It had rescued the slave from
oarbarism and had given him civilization and the Bible. Indeed,
ne insisted, it would be good for California. Happily, the
impossible demands of Davis for slavery where it had been
rejected by a large population were not shared by most Southerners in 1850, but he would be heard from again.

Northerners like William H. Seward, John Hale, Salmon P.
Chase, and others, opposed the Compromise as vehemently as
had Davis. Seward, the sophisticated and inconsistent politician,
spoke eloquently for this group when he denounced slavery as
a sin against God's law, a "higher law" than the American
Constitution. To the Seward of 1850 all legislative compromises
were "radically wrong and essentially vicious," involving the
"surrender of the exercise of judgment and conscience." Ob-
jecting to all compromise, Seward assailed this one in particular.
It would, he said, exchange human freedom in other areas for
"liberty, gold, and power on the Pacific coast." Seward struck
boldly at the South's most sacred dogma. The Constitution,
he said, did not really recognize property in slaves at all,
because in both the three-fifths clause and the provision regard-

ing the return of fugitives from labor, the Constitution used
the word "persons." Indeed, argued Seward, slavery should
not even be allowed to dominate the slave states, because in all
of them freedom was a more important institution than slavery
and the slaveholders were a disproportionate minority. Slavery
was "only a temporary, accidental, partial, and incongruous"
institution, while freedom was a "perpetual, organic, universal"
one, in harmony with the Constitution." And finally, avowed
Seward, the founding fathers had permitted slavery only because it already existed. None of them would have voted to
establish it anywhere. Indeed, no slave state with a choice would
have founded slavery. Slave state leaders themselves had established freedom throughout the Northwest Territory. Britain,
France, and Mexico had abolished it, and the rest of Europe
was following suit: slavery was incompatible with all the
world's best ideals and must not be established again anywhere.

Seward had struck the note which lacerated Southern feelings
most—a moral disapproval backed by world opinion and based
upon ideals shared by the South, and a refusal to grant Southerners even a shred of moral defense. Actually, Seward was
entirely tolerant toward slavery where it existed, but Southerners found his bland assumption of moral superiority well-
nigh unendurable. Obviously, Seward's point, which he himself
did not really believe, that all legislative compromises were
sinful could only mean rough days ahead.

Between the extremes of Calhoun and Seward were those
who saw the necessity for compromise and welcomed Clay's
high-minded idealism. Most of these, however, were determined
to push for every advantage and save as much face as possible
within the framework of Clay's proposals.

Most flexible was the proposition concerning New Mexico,

nd a substantial group of Southerners led by Henry Foote
ought to control this question by combining all the measures
n a single bill. By this they hoped to make a free California
he price for amendments favorable to Texas and an insurance
policy for the passage of the fugitive slave act. In the words
of South Carolina's Andrew P. Butler:

The great object to be attained was this . . . there were three vessels
at sea—one of them (California) was strong enough to carry the
other and weaker vessels into port, if connected with her. California
was a large and safe ship, and the other smaller boats in danger were
to be attached to her, and she would carry them all safely into port.

In 1839 Foote had toured Texas and had written a two-
volume history entitled *Texas and the Texans*. By 1850 he was
second only to the Texans themselves in working for the
annexation of New Mexico by Texas. Small, bald, and fiery,
Foote had fought four duels and had been shot down in three
of them. His exploits also included a rough-and-tumble fight
with his Mississippi colleague, Jefferson Davis, and a wrestling
match in the Senate aisle with the larger Senator Cameron of
Pennsylvania. Offering the motion to admit the ladies to the
gallery was part of his daily ritual, and he was always ready to
provide them with a performance. Foote's overall influence was
for the compromise, and his strategy for getting the maximum
advantage for Texas was sound. His methods, however, contributed little to sectional peace.

Determined to save New Mexico, Thomas Hart Benton led
those insisting that Clay's propositions must be dealt with singly.
At first Clay himself agreed, and he and Benton, longtime
enemies, were seen openly conferring. Foote, however, unmer-
cifully taunted Clay for "forgetting the animosities of thirty
years" and for treachery to the South. The sick and weary Clay

111

saw that a combination was the best hope for Southern support and finally agreed to support a move for a committee to write a single omnibus compromise bill.

For six long weeks the Senate argued over whether or not to form the committee. During these debates Foote attempted daily to provoke Benton into a physical attack. Over and over he taunted his older colleague with charges of falsehood, dishonor, and cowardice. Vice-President Fillmore refused to call Foote to order, and the normally hot-tempered Benton was remarkably patient. The inevitable day finally came, however, when the ponderous Benton rose and marched toward Foote. Foote drew a revolver and retreated down the aisle. "I have no pistols!" shouted Benton. "Let him fire! Stand out of the way. Let the assassin fire!" In the excitement a few Senators remained sensible enough to get between the antagonists. Benton was stopped, and Foote surrendered the pistol.

An investigating committee later absolved Foote of murderous intent, but charged that he had "without . . . provocation, indulged in personalities . . . of the most offensive character . . . calculated to rouse the fiercest resentment in the human bosom." For most Northerners Foote's performance illustrated the violent nature of men corrupted by slavery. "ASSASSIN FOOTE," shouted the Northern press, and the event would be long remembered.

Foote later announced he would write a small book in which Benton would play a very prominent role. Benton answered that he would write a very big book in which Foote would play no role whatever. Each kept his word.

The omnibus committee was finally created, and after three weeks it produced a fair bill. For twelve more hot, bitter, weary weeks, the Congress debated amendment after amend-

ient. Seward's group sought to add the Wilmot Proviso to the
erritories, while the Southerners tried one measure after an-
ther designed to give more of New Mexico to Texas. For-
unately, the Texas senators, Houston and Rusk, were Union
nen. They filled the air with pleas for justice, but they were
ntirely unwilling to create a dangerous showdown.

For some leaders political advantage was almost as important
s reaching a settlement. Seward had a commanding influence
vith President Taylor, who wanted the immediate admission
f a free California and the abandonment of the Texas claims
gainst New Mexico. The presidential patronage was going to
he Sewardites instead of to Vice-President Millard Fillmore,
lso of New York. Animosities toward Seward in both North
nd South became animosities also against the President, and
Taylor responded with still greater efforts against the Compro-
nise. This problem, however, was suddenly eliminated.

On July 4, the day after he had threatened to hang his
Southern Whig friends and lead an army against Texas, Presi-
lent Taylor attended a celebration at the partly finished
Washington Monument. He sat in the hot sun through an
extremely long speech by Henry Foote, after which he slaked
his thirst with great quantities of ice water and ate a few bowls
of cherries with cold milk—which was probably germ-laden.
After five days of suffering he was dead. The official diagnosis
vas typhoid fever.

The slaveholding Taylor had valiantly defended the Northern position, and he was a stronger President than his colleagues
had expected, but his untimely death in 1850 probably helped
America avoid civil war. The new President, Fillmore, hated
Seward and was strong for the compromise. His favors would
go to those accepting his version of patriotic reasonableness.

The Death of Slavery

After twenty-three more days of rancorous debate, the Senate suddenly passed amendments which split the omnibus bill into separate parts. The feeble Clay left for a needed seashore vacation, and Stephen A. Douglas of Illinois took command of the compromise. One at a time the measures passed much as Clay had proposed them. Texas abandoned its New Mexico claims, and the United States assumed $10,000,000 worth of Texas debts. The promised funds effectively smothered the Texas war talk.

·The Southern disunion convention at Nashville, meanwhile, had been a failure. Most Americans both north and south wanted compromise and peace in 1850. Ordinary Southerners still could not easily identify antislave restrictions in far-off territories as a threat of Northern violence against slavery in the Southern states. Webster's talk of a future which belonged to the free states and his plea against the useless reenactment of divine laws had struck a responsive chord in the average Northern heart. Both sections were immensely prosperous, and the whole country was enjoying a new era of productive expansion. The riches of a vast continent were still beckoning to a people learning more and more new ways to use them. There were wildernesses to be conquered, farms to be created, towns and cities to be built, and forests, mines, and pastures to be exploited. Railroads and even newer modes of transportation would soon be needed. It was a land of matchless opportunity, and men everywhere rejoiced that the crippling disease of the slavery quarrel had been at least temporarily arrested. Compromise leaders, with the exception of Webster, returned home as heroes, and unionists in both North and South won most of the 1851 elections. Running on a Union platform, Foote defeated Jefferson Davis for the governorship of Mississippi.

Retreat from the Abyss

Even in South Carolina the unionists could still be heard, and those who would take action only in cooperation with other southern states outnumbered those willing to go it alone.

The disease, however, was only arrested and not cured. The territory stretching from Texas to Canada and west of Missouri and Iowa remained unsettled. Slavery was apparently barred from the area by the laws of nature, but this did not eliminate the area as a further testing ground for Southern rights and Northern opposition to an alleged Slave Power. A fugitive slave act had been passed, but this did not mean that all Northerners would willingly surrender or help capture freedom-bound fugitives. The two-party system and the democratic process had been badly damaged. Personal hatreds and competitive animosities had received a further push. More elections and more clashes of ambitious politicians seeking votes and power lay ahead. New events would soon continue the process whereby the politicians' quarrel shared by only a minority in 1850 would become the peoples' war of 1861.

VIII

Some Ran Away

It is your privilege to catch your own slaves, if any
one catches them. . . . When you ask us to pay the
expenses of arresting your slaves, or to give the
President authority to appoint officers to do that
dirty work, give them power to compel our officers
to give chase to the panting bondman, you overstep
the bounds of the Constitution, and there we meet
you, and there we stand and there we shall remain.
We shall protest against such indignity; we shall
proclaim our abhorrence of such a law. Nor can
you seal or silence our voices.

JOSHUA GIDDINGS, 1852

On an October day in 1850, young William Craft and his
wife Ellen stood on the deck of a steamer and watched Boston
fade into the distance. They knew little of the England to
which they were bound, but their experiences since escaping
from a Georgia plantation two years earlier gave them reason
to expect kindness and generosity. They possessed enormous

ourage, and the slender, thin-faced girl was gifted with histri-
nic abilities akin to genius. They had stolen clothes and money,
nd with the light-skinned Ellen masquerading as a young
lanter accompanied by William, her slave, they had made their
ay openly by train from Georgia to the North. The master
nd officials who had come to arrest them had met threats and
ntimidation from a vigilance committee headed by Theodore
arker and were still unaware of their flight by sea. If the
rafts felt nostalgia, it was known to them alone, but after the
ivil War they would return voluntarily to Georgia.

In September, 1851, a Maryland slaveholder named Gorsuch
as killed and his son was seriously wounded when they tried
o recapture two slaves at Christiana, Pennsylvania. The slaves
scaped. Several negroes and two whites were arrested for
urder and treason. All were acquitted.

In June, 1854, fifty thousand hissing, groaning, and shouting
eople lined the streets of Boston as more than a thousand
eavily armed soldiers, marines, and police escorted a trembling
ave named Anthony Burns to a ship waiting to return him to
irginia. The cost of the capture was estimated at $100,000.

On January 27, 1856, Margaret Garner, her four children,
er husband and husband's parents, and nine other friends
alked across the frozen Ohio River to freedom. The friends
scaped to Canada. The Garners were surrounded at the home
f a kinsman. When all hope was lost, Margaret attacked her
hildren with a knife, killing one and wounding the others.
was said that the dead little girl was very beautiful and almost
hite. The recovery of the Garners cost $21,456 in payments
o four hundred marshals and became a major issue in Ohio
olitics.

On the night of December 20, 1858, John Brown led two

small raiding parties into Missouri. They directly and forcibl
abducted twelve slaves from their masters' premises. One maste
was shot to death. The affair was widely publicized, and
$3,000 reward was offered for Brown's capture. Brown led th
slaves almost twenty-five hundred miles through Kansas, N
braska, Iowa, Illinois, Indiana and Michigan. On March 12, 185
they crossed from Detroit into Canada. The efforts of Willia
P. Clark of Iowa City and J. B. Grinnell of Grinnell, Iowa, ha
enabled them to ride a closed railway freight car from We
Liberty, Iowa, to Chicago, but most of the journey was in th
open. For this exploit Brown was never arrested.

There were other spectacular incidents, but not many. Fe
were needed, however, to convince Southerners everywhe
that the North was filled with enemies blind to the Constitutio
and to all the laws of property. They were ultimately convince
that millions of dollars in slaves were being lost annually t
Northern criminality.

Slavery as an institution was as remote to the average Nort
erner of 1850 as Russian Communism is to the average twentiet
century American, but an individual fugitive risking life an
limb for freedom in 1850 was as real as an iron curtain refug
would be a century later. The very fact of running awa
appeared adequate proof of physical mistreatment, and whe
this was not true, the implication of an even greater spiritu
torture aroused equal sympathy. Fugitives who had lived
obscure safety in Northern towns for several years prior
1850 suddenly found themselves endangered—and just as su
denly found themselves with many new friends determined
defy the South's new law.

The 1850 law was uniquely designed to inflame Northe
consciences. Marshals or deputies could be fined $1,000 for no

ooperation with a pursuing master, and any person helping a
ugitive could be fined $1,000, imprisoned six months, and
ssessed $1,000 in civil damages for each slave escaping through
is efforts. For obvious reasons the fugitives were provided no
ury trial, and a claimant's affidavit was usually sufficient evi-
ence of title. Hearings were conducted by federal commis-
ioners, who received $10 if the fugitive was awarded to the
naster, but only $5 in case of a release. There is no evidence
hat any commissioner ever enslaved a free man for the extra $5,
ut the legalized temptation only made sharper the Northern
iew of the tyrannical and corrupting power of the Southern
lavocracy.

The new law quickly brought to a peak of organization the
Underground Railroad system whereby Northerners in almost
very state organized their efforts to help the fugitives. Circu-
ating information among slaves and sending former fugitives
ack to the South as leaders, organizers, and guides; hiding
ugitives in secret rooms, basements, churches, barns, caves,
nd thickets; and transporting them by night and day through
ll manner of ingenious ruses, more than three thousand North-
rners at one time or another helped slaves make their way from
Southern plantations and homes to Canada.

Assuredly, the significance of even one human being seeking
reedom cannot be taken lightly, but the extent of the fear,
itterness, and hatred between the sections generated by the
ugitive slave problem rested in part upon a gross exaggeration
f the numbers involved. The United States census indicates
hat the annual loss was less than 1 per 5,000 slaves. In 1859, 803
laves escaped, and 500 of these were from border states. The
order states, which suffered most of the losses, showed little
xcitement. The Deep South, from which escape was almost

The Death of Slavery

impossible and which lost a mere handful—only 16 of the 400,000 slaves in South Carolina escaped in 1850—was in constant fury over the allegedly massive Northern depredations. Similarly, in the border states of the North to which all slaves had to escape at first and in which most of the recapture occurred, protest was at a minimum. In far-off New England, Michigan, and Wisconsin, where slave-catchers were almost never seen, the press, politicians, and pulpit kept up a constant din against Southern kidnapers. At least one historian of the Underground Railway has judged from the boasting of ex-Railroad workers and the depth of Southern anguish that the census figures reveal only a fraction of the actual losses. The figures were provided by Southerners, however, and it is unlikely that people who were publicly broadcasting their grievances at every opportunity would have minimized them when dealing with the census-takers.

The fugitive slave issue apparently developed no great zeal on the part of most Northerners to attack the South with physical force. It did, however, increase Northern determination against humoring the South with concessions, however meaningless, in the remaining territories, and it helped prepare Northerners to believe the worst of any charges made against the South. The cost of regaining a slave was frequently greater than his value, and the commercial value of the known runaway was immediately depreciated. Every Northern act of assistance to a runaway, however, was by implication a moral condemnation of the institution and the South itself. This, rather than the actual economic losses, probably caused the greatest Southern fear and anger. The question contributed much to the ultimate Southern secession. The creation of a separate Southern nation would only move the freedom line from Canada down to the

Some Ran Away

Ohio River, but the illogicality of this solution struck few secessionists in 1860.

It is remarkable that such a dramatic and emotional theme as the struggles of people to escape slavery produced only one major work of literature, but it is natural that the book which gained a virtual monopoly of the subject should have enjoyed such an enormous popularity.

If Harriet Beecher Stowe had no authentic experience with Southern masters, plantations, or slaves, she had considerable contact with fugitives. *Uncle Tom's Cabin* was her first literary venture, but she was gifted with the ability to breathe life into her characters from the moment they spoke. The aspirations, fears, sufferings, frustrations, nobility, and villainies of her characters can still be felt intensely by every reader. The book quickly became an all-time best seller, and as far away as Russia masters liberated their serfs after reading it. It showed slavery at its worst, and put countless readers into the shoes and skins of the slaves themselves. Southerners pointed out in vain that in real life situations and events such as hers rarely if ever happened, because it was clear that everything in the book was entirely possible. Despite Mrs. Stowe's conscious effort to avoid condemning Southerners as such, the Yankee-born overseer, Simon Legree, became a cruel stereotype of the Southern slaveholder. Similarly, the saintly Uncle Tom, the heroic George Harris and Eliza, and the delightful Topsy became the typical slaves in the minds and emotions of Northern readers.

Critics have argued that Mrs. Stowe exaggerated the virtues and capacities of the average slave at this particular stage of his cultural development, and a few still attribute this alleged backwardness to innate racial inferiority. Others, with far more logic and evidence, blame it upon the crippling effects of

121

slavery itself. Some have suggested that the unfortunately premature investment of the still uneducated and inexperienced Negro with great political power in the South during Reconstruction was due in large part to the excessively optimistic view of his superior nature as taught by *Uncle Tom's Cabin.* Another recent author, however, insists that Mrs. Stowe with all her good intentions was essentially a racist who helped create unfavorable stereotypes of Negro character that still plague his quest for legal and social equality. This argument cites her paternalistic attitude, but draws most of its evidence from the later plays and "Tom" shows that were only remotely based upon her original story. Among the slaves' descendants at least, Uncle Tom has come half circle from his original status as a slave hero to a symbol of cowardly acquiescence to white indignities.

Whatever the later judgments, the book was a major spur to sectional conflict. It strengthened the righteous resolve of Northerners to help fugitives and to insist upon legal barriers against slavery in the territories, however unsuited for slavery they might be. Its enormous popularity contributed much to the growing Southern paranoia. Being out of step with the civilized world on a great moral question is deeply painful, and many Southerners, if only subconsciously, must have recognized the conflict between the noble ideals supporting their own right to freedom and their convictions about slavery. Fanatical zeal is often the product of profound doubt and insecurity.

IX

Bleeding Kansas and Bleeding Sumner

On a balmy afternoon in June, 1852, Mr. and Mrs. Franklin Pierce were enjoying a leisurely carriage ride through the pleasant New England countryside near Boston when a friend galloped up with exciting news. After the better-known leaders

123

like Douglas, Cass, Buchanan, Marcy, and Butler had been exhausted by the struggles against each other, the Democratic national convention on the forty-eighth ballot had nominated Franklin Pierce for President of the United States. Mrs. Pierce listened intently to the messenger and then fainted dead away.

Several months later, President-elect and Mrs. Pierce and their only child, an eleven-year-old son, were still savoring their triumph as they rode along on a train from Boston to Concord. Suddenly the car lurched and tumbled down an embankment. Young Benjamin Pierce died before his horrified parents' eyes. His mother never fully regained her sanity, and social life at the White House during the Pierce regime was almost non-existent.

The problems of a grieving, suffering wife did not make President Pierce's job easier, and he was at best ill-equipped for its responsibilities. His rivals for the nomination had fallen one by one because each had well-known convictions and the enemies that went with them. Pierce had neither deep convictions nor enemies, but he would soon correct the latter deficiency. John Letcher wrote Pierce that he confidently expected protection for the South. On the same day, David Wilmot wrote the new President his expectation that Pierce would check the South.

For a candidate the Whigs had again turned to a military hero, General Winfield Scott. Henry Clay was dying, attended in his illness by Mrs. Francis P. Blair. The Blairs had loved Clay in their youth, but had later fought him bitterly for twenty-five years. In his final days, the old Kentuckian achieved mutual forgiveness and reconciliation with the Blairs, Van Buren, and Thomas Hart Benton in turn, as the old enmities faded into insignificance beside the new perils facing the American Union. Daniel Webster had hoped for a final chance, but he too was

nearing death, with the voices of countless erstwhile admirers
still calling curses down upon his vote for the fugitive slave bill.
Nominated by a party split in half by the fugitive slave act,
Scott was overwhelmed by Pierce at the polls, and the Whigs
had no national leader to replace Clay and Webster. Northern
and Southern Whigs would henceforth go their separate ways,
each in search of a new allegiance. The Whig party died with
Scott's vanishing hopes, and its efforts for national unity would
be sorely missed.

If the Compromise of 1850 was to endure, its defenders would
need all possible help from the White House. Unionists North
and South had won most of the 1851–52 elections, and Pierce
might well have been expected to strengthen their hands with
his major appointments. Radicals and moderates of both sections begged for cabinet posts and equated the President's kindly
words with commitments. In the end, however, Pierce ignored
the unionist friends of Douglas in the Northwest and the recently victorious Southern moderates. Instead, he bowed to
Southern extremists with two appointments totally lacking in
political wisdom. Jefferson Davis, recently defeated by a conservative unionist for governor of Mississippi, became Secretary
of War. Caleb Cushing, highly talented, but despised in his
native Massachusetts because of pro-Southern sympathies, became Attorney General. The two soon came to dominate their
leader. In diplomatic appointments also, Pierce gave the plums
to extremist Southerners and their friends. Union men everywhere, and especially in the South, felt deserted by the Democratic party and its new administration.

The Southern influence in foreign affairs was quickly felt. In
late 1853 Pierce in the Gadsden Treaty gave Santa Anna $10,-
000,000 for a narrow strip of desert south of Arizona and New

The Death of Slavery

Mexico. The land was considered worthless, and the only obvious reason for the purchase was to gain a right-of-way for
new railroad from California to New Orleans or Memphis. The
treaty roused angry Northern opposition.

In October, 1854, the longtime Southern dream of a new
slave state in Cuba flowered in the famous Ostend manifesto
American ministers Buchanan from England, Mason from
France, and Soulé from Spain, met in Belgium to issue a public
offer to buy Cuba coupled with an open threat to take it by
force if necessary. Spanish anger was exceeded only by that of
American Northerners, and the project was hastily disavowed
by the administration.

Meanwhile, in January, 1854, Northern anger at the South
had agained reached a new height.

Stephen A. Douglas, the Little Giant from Illinois, was five
feet four, almost as wide as high, and a tough, ruthless political
battler. He intended to be President some day, and though only
forty he was not one for extended waiting. He knew what the
slave issue had done to the Whig party, and he hoped to save
his own Democrats from a similar fate. His political future as
well as his hopes for a growing, united America required a
slavery formula upon which Northern and Southern Democrats
could agree.

Douglas was also a land speculator with enormous faith in
the future of his home city of Chicago. Obviously the eastern
end of the California railroad should be in Chicago. The senator
was also chairman of the Committee on Territories. It was his
duty to get territories organized, and lying in the path of his
proposed railroad route to California was the vast area to become Kansas and Nebraska. A railroad through these virgin
regions would require liquidation of Indian titles, new terri-

orial governments, and occupation by the usual horde of
rontiersmen waiting for new lands. A bill for these purposes
almost passed in March, 1853, and by December the situation
had become pressing. Southerners wanted a southern railroad
route, and Secretary of War Jefferson Davis already had the
army engineers surveying their way toward the new Gadsden
purchase. Closer home, former Senator and now Representative
Thomas Hart Benton was beating the drums for a route to St.
Louis, and the pictures of trade and intercourse with the Orient
painted by his soaring imagination and thunderous oratory had
roused people all over Missouri. Indeed, Benton had already
been to the Kansas border to make speeches urging Missourians
to force the territorial issue by moving into Kansas ahead of
any legal action.

Drafting a bill for organizing Kansas-Nebraska was routine,
but certain Southern leaders threatened opposition because the
territory would be automatically free under the provisions of
the Missouri Compromise of 1820. Particularly noisy was Senator David Atchison of Missouri. President of the Senate and
crude and forceful, Atchison was under pressure from Missouri
slaveholders anxious to avoid another neighboring haven for
fugitive slaves, and he could not accept a Kansas bill for which
the hated Benton might claim some of the credit. The bill must
provide a concession to Missouri slaveholders and if possible be
unacceptable to Benton. Atchison easily persuaded other
Southern senators, although the real depth of their opposition
to a bill which would not mention slavery is difficult to measure.
Some observers, including the not unprejudiced Benton and
one Abraham Lincoln, later insisted the matter had not disturbed the Southern people and that the measure could have
passed without disturbing the sacred compromise. Certainly,

continued obedience to a thirty-three year old law originally
passed with heavy Southern support could not be regarded as a
new insult to the South. Douglas, however, wanted a broad
Democratic consensus as well as a majority vote for his bill. He
was convinced that slavery could never go to either Kansas or
Nebraska, and believing most people to be equally realistic, he
concerned himself only with finding a face-saving solution for
all concerned.

The doctrine of popular sovereignty, or simply allowing the
territorial settlers to decide the matter of slavery for themselves, had occasioned no great criticism when first enunciated
by Lewis Cass in 1848 and later incorporated in limited form
in the Compromise of 1850. To Douglas it was the obvious
panacea. The Missouri Compromise, he hoped at first, could be
left unmentioned unless Southerners actually took slaves to
Kansas, and this he was certain would not happen.

The inconsistency between popular sovereignty and a federal
statute barring slavery, however, would not down. After days
of private arguments, Whig Senator Dixon of Kentucky on
January 15, 1854, offered an amendment repealing the Missouri
Compromise, and Douglas reluctantly accepted it. President
Pierce, weak and indecisive, listened to Jefferson Davis as well
as to Douglas and the Southern Senators. The administration
would support the repeal.

The realistic Douglas had not realized that others were less
realistic than himself. To the Northern public the repeal of the
Missouri Compromise looked too much like a Southern con-
spiracy to steal the great West for slavery. A group headed by
Salmon P. Chase, Charles Sumner, Benjamin Wade, and Gerrit
Smith immediately published "An Appeal of the Independent
Democrats in Congress to the People of the United States,"

which swept rapidly across the country in the press and pulpit. The "Appeal" was based upon the false premise that a prospective belt of midwestern slave states from Texas to Canada was about to rob all free men of their western birthright, but it found readers ready to believe the worst. The "Appeal" denounced this "gross violation of a sacred pledge; as a criminal betrayal of precious rights; as part and parcel of an atrocious plot to exclude from a vast unoccupied region, immigrants from the Old World and free laborers from our own States, and convert it into a dreary region of despotism, inhabited by masters and slaves."

In some of the fiercest parliamentary scenes in American history, Douglas fought back with the theme that all informed men knew that geography and climate barred slavery from the region.

At least two elderly statesmen agreed with Douglas but saw his mistake in its larger implications. The old Texas hero, Sam Houston, six feet six and tough as ever, stopped whittling and rose to spurn this alleged favor to his section. This useless measure, he said, would only convulse the country from Maine to the Rio Grande, and he would have no part of it. "If this repeal takes place," he warned, "I will have seen the commencement of the agitation, but the youngest child now born, will not live to witness its termination."

In the House, Houston's old commander and friend, Thomas Hart Benton, was even more explicit. Half the Union would be arrayed against the other in deadly hostility, he warned, and by an action suggested "not by the inhabitants—not by anyone living, or expecting to live in the territory . . . but by a motion in Congress—a silent, secret, limping, halting, creeping, squinting, impish motion, conceived in the dark—midwifed in a committee room, and sprung upon Congress and the country in the style in which Guy Fawkes intended to blow up the parliament house."

The two old comrades knew their America well. People, large and small, who cared little for the sufferings of the slave or the sins of his master, reacted violently against the possibility of a blighting slave desert blocking the access of free men to the Pacific. To northwesterners especially, the traitorous repeal of the Missouri Compromise was just another in a long line of wicked interferences by evil slavocrats in the glorious destiny of America which could be realized only when men like themselves had occupied the continent. And a further insult was added when the vociferous opposition of Germans and other immigrant groups led to an amendment denying aliens the right to vote or hold office in the new territory. Attacks on the bill by Northern newspapers, politicians, and preachers soon swelled into a new chorus of invective against the South itself, and their Southern counterparts, after a surprisingly long period of puzzled apathy, ultimately responded in kind.

After four months of name-calling and fierce debate, numerous supporters, including the President, wished they had never heard of Kansas, but Douglas kept them in line and the bill passed.

A few weeks earlier, Eli Thayer had launched what became the New England Emigrant Aid Society to send antislavery land-seekers to Kansas. Popular sovereignty would get an assist from the righteous. Dozens of similar companies appeared in various states, but Thayer's organization remained the prototype. At first, success came hard because Kansas, after all, was fifteen hundred miles away. In 1854–55 only 1,240 signed up, and Garrison complained that there was hardly an abolitionist among them. Then Kansas held its first territorial elections.

Bleeding Kansas and Bleeding Sumner

The Kansas-Missouri border had long been crowded with mule skinners, trail guides, trappers, Indian scouts, buffalo hunters, speculators, gun salesmen, and the usual run of lawless drifters and adventurers attracted to every frontier. It would perhaps be no coincidence that the only United States President produced by western Missouri would be noted for aggressive roughness. Such men had long considered Kansas their own, and excited in part by Benton's loud insistence that Indian titles were already clear enough to permit a settlement, they had almost reached the limits of patience before Douglas introduced his bill. Indeed, they had already crossed the border by the hundreds to stake out their future claims. Almost none of them owned any slaves, but they were mostly from the slave state of Missouri, and what was good enough for Old Mizzou was good enough for them. The continuation of the Missouri Compromise would not have affected their ambitions in the least, but its repeal made slavery legal if they wanted it. Missourians would demand every right coming to them whether they expected to use it or not. When word arrived that New England Yankees had organized a multimillion-dollar corporation to send abolitionists out to grab off the choice lands of Kansas, the cause of slavery suddenly assumed a symbolic value totally unrelated to economics. Frontier editors and politicians had no trouble whatever in rousing most of western Missouri into a state of armed alert.

Despite the noise, however, no serious problems developed beyond the usual barroom murders and conflicts over land claims, town sites, and county seats, until November, 1854, and March, 1855, when first a territorial delegate to Congress and then a territorial legislature had to be elected. By the end of 1854, the small number of slaves in Kansas, the widespread racist objections to the presence of any Negroes, whether slave

131

or free, and the obvious reluctance of slaveholding emigrants to risk Kansas when Arkansas and Texas also beckoned, had already indicated clearly that Kansas was destined to become a free state. Missourians, however, had their pride. In both elections a wild throng of Missourians, some of them half-drunk, crossed the border to vote. More than seventeen hundred Missourians voted in November, and a proslave delegate went to Congress. In March more than five thousand Missourians repeated the performance of November. Former Senator Atchison—the Bentonians had beaten him in the 1854 election—led eighty armed voters personally, and assured them there would be enough Missouri voters to "kill every God-damned abolitionist in the Territory."

Stealing an election, however, could not make Kansas a slave state. Indeed, the effect was the opposite. The almost defunct emigrant aid societies revived rapidly as word of these "slave power" outrages swept across the North. More and more Northerners poured into the region, but the actual patterns of conflict and violence differed but little from those on other frontiers. In fact, with somewhat less whisky and little talk of slavery, Iowans were sharing with equal enthusiasm in the early affairs of Nebraska. Kansas, however, was a battleground between nominal proslavers and crusaders for freedom, even though the crusaders themselves wrote a constitution which forbade forever the entry of any Negro—free or slave—into Kansas. Abolitionists who filled the United States Congress with passionate oratory in support of this constitution conveniently ignored this "black law" provision.

Kansas was quickly blessed with numerous newspaper correspondents ready to fight against slavery and squeeze the last drop of blood from "bleeding Kansas" for the benefit of their eastern readers. In the Northern press, every victim of violence, whether the affair involved a card game, romantic competition, claim-jumping, or just general orneriness, was a martyr for freedom at the hands of a mob of tobacco-chewing, whiskey-sodden, oath-breathing, depraved Southerners. The Southern press tried to respond in kind, but like their emigrant aid movement, such efforts never achieved much conviction. An essentially normal frontier struggle thus became bleeding Kansas, the first battle of the Civil War.

"I believed," wrote the abolitionist correspondent James Redpath, "that a civil war between the North and South would ultimate in [slave] insurrection, and that the Kansas troubles would probably create a military conflict. . . . Hence I . . . went to Kansas; and endeavored, personally and by my pen, to precipitate a revolution." In Redpath's reporting the cold-blooded murder and horrible mutilation by cutlasses of five alleged proslavers in one night by John Brown became a proslave outrage.

"I have no choice," said Brown to wavering followers. "It has been ordained by the Almighty God, ordained from eternity, that I should make an example of these men." For Redpath this explanation was entirely adequate. The famous "sack of Lawrence" caused only two casualties, both proslavers and both accidental victims of the excitement and free-flowing whiskey. In the Northern press the event became a major holocaust featuring, according to Redpath, pyramids of fire, the booming of cannon, two rapes, and two hundred stolen horses.

William A. Phillips of the *New York Tribune* went to Kansas "not only to write well, but also . . . to fight well." His book of what were essentially fairy tales, entitled *The Conquest of Kansas, by Missouri and Her Allies*, became a free state bible, and later made him a Kansas senator. Another reporter found reading his *Chicago Tribune* in the midst of the proslavers like reading the Scriptures in secret during the reign of Bloody Mary.

As the victims of Southern bestiality, including at least one young woman ravished and left for dead while returning from "one of the outbuildings in the rear of the house," continually multiplied in the Northern press, harsh criticisms of all things Southern increased proportionately. Bleeding Kansas was now ready to furnish the lifeblood for a new northern political party.

With regret I come again upon the Senator from South Carolina, who . . . overflows with rage at the simple suggestion that Kansas has applied for admission as a free state, and with incoherent phrases, discharges the loose expectoration of his speech, now upon her representatives, and then upon her people. There was no extravagance of the ancient, parliamentary debate which he did not respect, nor was there any possible deviation from truth which he did not make, with so much of passion, I gladly add, as to save him from the suspicion of intentional aberration.

Were the whole history of South Carolina blotted out of existence, from its very beginning down to the day of the last election of the senator . . . civilization might lose—I do not say how little; but surely less than it has already gained by the example of Kansas against oppression. Ah, Sir, I tell the senator that Kansas, welcomed as a free state, will be a ministering angel to the Republic when South Carolina, in the cloak of darkness which she hugs, lies howling.

The tall (six feet four), handsome speaker was Charles Sumner, Senator from Massachusetts, and the words were part of an eight-hour oration which generated great heat but shed little light upon the actual problems of Kansas. Senator Andrew Pickens Butler, the object of Sumner's special attention, was an elderly gentleman who, like most Southerners, frequently spoke strongly on sectional questions. He did not use abusive language, however, and off the floor he was popular with colleagues from both sections.

Sumner was a genuine idealist of great ability. He was also overbearing, egotistical, and self-righteous. His only marriage ended in failure after a few months—reportedly his bride could not stand living with God. Once, when told that Sumner did not believe in the Bible, Ulysses S. Grant, in a rare flash of wit, answered, "That's because he didn't write it." To Charles Francis Adams, Sumner was "a tremendous egotist and woefully lacking in common sense."

The attack upon Butler served no useful purpose. Freedom of speech and immunity from libel prosecution on the floors of Congress are necessary for a free, effective parliamentary government, but they presuppose a certain mature restraint on the part of the lawmakers. Even the most heinous accusation, if documented, can be offered in a reasonable and unemotional manner. "That damned fool will get himself killed by some other damned fool," said Stephen A. Douglas, himself ridiculed as "the Sancho Panza of slavery" in the speech.

The defense of family honor was and is more obligatory in Southern society than elsewhere in America, and Senator Butler had a young and vigorous nephew in the House of Representatives. After two days of brooding and sleepless nights, Representative Preston Brooks of South Carolina marched to the Senate floor and shattered his cane against the head of Senator Sumner.

The Senator was painfully hurt, but did not lose consciousness. Estimates of the number of blows ranged from six according to Southerners up to three dozen counted by observant Northerners. All agreed that the hollow, gutta-percha cane was destroyed beyond repair. Dr. Boyle reported two scalp wounds of approximately two inches each. One healed immediately but the other became infected. This was corroborated by Doctors Miller and Linsley, who reported much improvement in the infected wound after they had opened and drained it. At this point, Sumner's brother and Dr. Perry from Boston took charge of the case. The ailing Senator was taken to the Silver Spring plantation of Francis Preston Blair, where, presumably, he was cared for by Blair's slaves, and alarming bulletins about his condition began appearing regularly.

The earlier doctors' description of Sumner's swollen lymph glands indicates that he probably did suffer an extreme crisis from infection, but it is equally likely that a rapid cure ensued once the initial infection was overcome. Sumner, however, did not return to the Senate for three and a half years. During this long period he toured Europe seeking medical assistance. His travels were spiced by a social life of furious energy, and included a traversing of the Alps on muleback because he felt too weak to walk. "I have been in the Pyrenees, in the Alps, and in the Channel Isles," he wrote a friend. "You will next hear of me in the Highlands of Scotland." A Parisian doctor diagnosed the ailment as a sprained spine which caused deep pain with each deep thought or emotion. Modern students of psychosomatic illness would have understood Sumner's problems.

The extent of Sumner's injury, however, is of academic interest. More important, a personal brawl due to an insult to an aged relative quickly became another national struggle between slavery and freedom. Massachusetts offered to pay all medical bills, to which Sumner replied, "Let whatever Massachusetts can give go to suffering Kansas." Yale and Amherst granted the Harvard-educated statesman honorary degrees.

"The surgeons of the City of Washington," was the toast of

Bleeding Kansas and Bleeding Sumner

Oliver Wendell Holmes at a medical society dinner. "God grant them wisdom for they are dressing the wounds of a mighty empire and of countless generations." The *New York Tribune* echoed the spirit of hundreds of public meetings attended by throngs of angry and excited Northerners: "A thorough-going and consistent advocate of slavery would not scruple at a lie or false oath or hesitate at murder." Beecher, Evarts, Wayland, Emerson, Everett, and Bryant brought excited crowds to the point of hysteria with their descriptions of the attempted assassination. To the British minister, Cornwell Lewis, it was "the first blow in a civil war." Bleeding Sumner had joined bleeding Kansas.

In the South, Brooks was widely criticized for making the Senate floor an arena, but it was generally agreed that Sumner deserved the caning. After the Northern press had vilified Brooks as an assassin and described his act as typical of the slaveholding morality, the South rallied to his defense. New canes, at least one inscribed "Hit him again," were sent to Brooks, and editorials and resolutions praising his "act of justice" appeared all over the South.

The Northerners had their own heroic bully boy in Senator Benjamin Franklin Wade, a tough frontier type from Ohio. Wade insulted Southerners and the South in language even more direct than that of Sumner. When challenged to a duel, Bluff Ben chose squirrel rifles at twenty paces with each man to pin a white piece of paper over his heart. The challenging Southerner denounced Wade as a barbarian and no gentleman, and the duel was never fought. For the rest of the decade, Wade roamed the Congress like a modern Goliath, taunting his colleagues and daring any and all comers to physical combat—and, strangely enough, finding no Southern David willing to accept his terms. In 1858, Wade, Simon Cameron of Pennsylvania, and Zachariah Chandler of Michigan announced a compact whereby they would make the personal quarrels of any offended Northern colleague their own. For some Southerners the prospect of a new Southern senate without Wade in it may have been a subconscious force working for secession.

By 1856, the personal antagonisms in Washington itself, the demise of the Whig party and the need of commerce and industry for a party, the rage of Northern Democrats who felt betrayed by the Kansas affair, the lingering resentments of Free-Soil elements left from 1848, and the longtime hope of the abolitionists for influence in a major party had combined to produce a new Republican party. The party began with various fusion movements in several Northern states in 1854, and by 1856 it was ready for a national convention. Francis Preston Blair, slaveholder, Free-Soiler, and former editor and aide to Andrew Jackson, served as chairman, and the delegates in the convention hall included men who had been his enemies for a quarter of a century. Democrats like Blair, Preston King, Salmon P. Chase, and William Cullen Bryant were now ready for common cause with Whigs like Seward, Thurlow Weed, Thad Stevens, and Horace Greeley.

The Blairs were powerful in the new party, and the 1856 candidate was their choice. John C. Frémont had played an exaggerated but well-published role in opening the Oregon trail and conquering California, and he had been a martyr in the hated administration of James K. Polk. The fact that he had deserved his court-martial was irrelevant. The dashing "Pathfinder," born in Georgia and reared in South Carolina, was an outspoken enemy of slavery and slave-expansion, and his father-in-law was the still popular ex-Senator Benton. A Whiggish economic program headed by the slogan "Free Soil and Free Men" was the Frémont platform.

The Democrats convened in Cincinnati, with Douglas eager for the nomination but still young enough to wait. There was a free-for-all fist fight between two competing Missouri delegations, but Northern and Southern Democrats ultimately found harmony in the nomination of James Buchanan. By spending four years as minister to England, the Pennsylvanian had avoided the battles which had weakened the other aspirants. The two bitter enemies, Douglas and Benton, each saw hope in Buchanan.

A third party was in the field in 1856. There was brutal competition for jobs in the burgeoning new Northern mills and factories, and efforts to gain better wages and working conditions were weakened by the seemingly inexhaustible supply of cheap immigrant labor. Unions were as yet almost non-existent, and an attempt to turn the law of supply and demand to the benefit of labor by restricting immigration appeared to be a logical solution. Also, of course, many of the newcomers were Roman Catholics. Authors and publishers willing to promote hatred and suspicion at a profit were not lacking, and the vicious nonsense in their books and pamphlets provided a moral justification for cruelties dictated primarily by self-interest. In the mid-1850's, various American cities suffered bloody riots in which helpless immigrants were murdered in cold blood by nativist mobs. By 1856 this combination of fear and bigotry had produced the American or Know-Nothing party, which drew most of its organizational strength from the former Whigs. The Democratic rank and file were also seriously affected, although the Democratic party remained firmly on record against such tactics and was clearly identified in many areas as the party of the immigrant. A substantial number of immigrants, especially the Germans, were also strongly attracted by the Republican platform against slavery extension.

Meeting in convention, the Know-Nothings nominated former President Millard Fillmore, who had never been a member of their party and who could not even be consulted because of his absence in Europe. Fillmore, personally the antithesis of fanaticism, persuaded himself that the party could become a new political home for conservative Whigs unwilling to join the Republicans and a new rallying point for national unity. Presumably, Northerners and Southerners were to submerge their slavery conflict in a common front against a greater danger —the prospect of America's inundation and destruction by a horde of Catholic workers dedicated to betraying America into the hands of the Pope. The platform accepted popular sovereignty as a solution to the slavery quarrel.

In 1856, therefore, America's presidential choices were a dashing hero lacking in common sense but running on a platform in step with democracy's highest ideals; a former President campaigning from the best of motives but representing a party dedicated to the worst of human emotions; and a professional politician hitherto noted only for indecisiveness and subservience to Southern interests.

Frémont was not even on the ballot in the South, and the fire-eaters spread the alarm far and wide. The election of a Free-Soil President, they argued, would leave the South no honorable alternative but secession. Calmer Southerners pleaded that their section had as yet suffered no real indignities and that even if Frémont were elected, he should be given every opportunity to prove that he meant the South no harm. Whether the ordinary Southerner believed the frightening predictions of so many of his leaders cannot be determined. He continued with his business and voted for Buchanan.

In keeping with the spirit of the times, both Democrats and Know-Nothings charged that Frémont was a Catholic. In 1841, Frémont had bowed to the will of his seventeen-year-old fiancée, Jessie Benton, and consented to an elopement. After several Protestant ministers, probably fearful of the wrath of the bride's father, Senator Benton, had refused to perform the ceremony, the young lovers had found a brave Catholic priest. The record of this Catholic ceremony was adequate proof for Frémont's opponents, and Frémont, who moreover had much strength among immigrant voters, did not dignify the charge with a denial.

Frémont's father-in-law, Benton, was still popular, and his expected support had been an argument for Frémont's nomination. Old Bullion, however, sadly parted company with his favorite daughter and son-in-law. In a forty-day period, the old man delivered twenty speeches calling for the election of Buchanan—whom he personally detested. America, he said, must not elect a purely sectional President, or a civil war would follow.

Fierce animosities are a by-product of the competition of every American national election, and 1856 produced even more than its share. The war in Kansas shared headlines with the presidential candidates, and for Republicans Frémont was the Galahad who alone could save the territory and the West in general from slavery. Frémont attracted to his banner some of the purest idealism ever generated in American politics, but in the end too many Americans recognized the dangers which would follow his election. The national candidate, James Buchanan, was elected, but Frémont ran a powerful second with

114 electoral votes to the victor's 174. Buchanan carried only five of the sixteen free states, and Frémont had a popular edge of more than 100,000 votes over Buchanan in the free states. Southerners were left painfully aware that without the Know-Nothings Frémont might have been elected, and that a few shifts here and there might easily elect a Republican in 1860.

X

The Political Quest for
Peace and Votes

> I would give them any legislation for the reclaim-
> ing of their fugitives, which should not . . . be more
> likely to carry a free man into slavery, than our
> ordinary criminal laws are to hang an innocent
> one. . . . If we could arrest the spread, and place
> it where . . . it *would be* in the course of ultimate
> extinction, and the public mind *would* . . . believe
> that it was in the course of ultimate extinction, the
> crisis would be past and the institution might be
> left alone for a hundred years, if it should live so
> long, in the States where it exists.
>
> ABRAHAM LINCOLN

James Buchanan was not a particularly happy man. Many years
before, his fiancée had died suddenly under mysterious circumstances while the young Buchanan was on an extended
business trip to another city, and her parents had forbidden him

to attend the funeral. His neglect was allegedly related to the tragedy, and for this real or imagined cruelty the young man had vowed to atone by remaining faithful to her memory for the rest of his life. As a Washington bachelor he gravitated naturally to the gay, convivial Southerners who most often left their own wives at home. For many years fellow bachelor William R. King of Alabama was his best friend. Lacking any deep convictions on political issues, and apparently with no moral antipathy toward slavery, Buchanan all too often allowed his personal affections for individual Southerners to determine his political actions.

The new President's road was made no easier by the final message of the retiring Franklin Pierce. Bitter over his own rejection, Pierce lashed out at the Republicans as radical fanatics bent upon destroying America with a bloody race war. The congressional session preceding Buchanan's inauguration was spent largely in rancorous debates over the justice or injustice of Pierce's accusations. When Buchanan appointed Southerners to most of the important cabinet posts, the anger left by Pierce boiled again to the surface.

James Buchanan, hater of controversy, grasped for straws of peace in his inaugural address. Popular sovereignty, he said, was a fair solution to the territorial problem, and the Supreme Court would soon rule on the question of just when the settlers could make their fateful decision on slavery. Almost petulantly he begged Americans to accept the decision of the Court, turn away from conflict, and get on with the more important business of developing America.

If Buchanan had any previous knowledge of the expected Court opinion, his address showed an abysmal ignorance of the Northern public mind. The Dred Scott decision ignored both

Northern sentiment and all precedents related to the principle it sought to establish. It was also perhaps the most unnecessary opinion ever rendered by an American court.

Ostensibly the freedom of slave Dred Scott was at stake. In reality all parties concerned had long since agreed that he was to go free as soon as his usefulness as a liberty-seeker should be ended. Scott had lived in the free state of Illinois and the free territory of Wisconsin as the slave of army surgeon John Emerson. After returning voluntarily with his wife and children to St. Louis with the doctor, Scott found himself in difficult straits after his master died and the widow could no longer support a slave and his family. After supporting the Scotts for some time, the son of a former owner finally financed Dred in a suit for freedom on the grounds that residence in the free areas had made him free. The first trial went against Scott. The second ended in his favor. By this time the territorial quarrel gave the case a new meaning. Mrs. Emerson went to Massachusetts and married an abolitionist. Rather than simply grant Scott his freedom, she transferred him by a fictitious sale to a brother, who went through the motions of resisting Scott's pleas until the case reached the Supreme Court of the United States.

The Court, headed by the venerable Roger B. Taney, a former radical Jacksonian Democrat, at first decided that the status of a slave in Scott's circumstances should be decided by the courts of the slave state. This opinion was supported by numerous earlier precedents, but Justices McLean and Curtis submitted long dissents covering the entire question of territorial slavery. In response to McLean and Curtis, Taney and the majority, none of them slaveholders, produced a long discourse covering the same ground, although the actual verdict remained unchanged.

The Death of Slavery

Taney argued in effect that no Negro could be a citizen, and that Scott, therefore, could not sue in a federal court. Since citizenship was still a matter of state jurisdiction, this judgment was entirely unwarranted. Then Taney lit a fuse. The Congress had been ruling territories as it saw fit since the Northwest Ordinance of 1787, and this power had always been accepted by the courts, the Congress, and the people alike. Taney, however, ruled that the Constitution followed the flag—that the citizens of any American territory, regardless of its qualifications for statehood, had the same constitutional rights, obligations, and powers as the citizens of the existing states. Slaves, he reasoned further, were recognized as property in the Constitution, the Constitution decreed that no citizen could be deprived of property without due process of law, and the Congress, therefore, could not bar slavery in any territory. The already dead Missouri Compromise had been unconstitutional from the beginning.

The Dred Scott decision did not put a single slave in a single western territory, and later courts reversed its basic principle in dealing with overseas territories. It returned Scott to slavery, but he was immediately set free and in fact finished his life as a hotel porter. For many Americans in 1857, however, the ruling seemed just another step in the onward rush of the slave power to spread the wicked institution across the continent. Republicans still smarting from the denunciations of Pierce and angry over Buchanan's pro-Southern leanings remembered the President's inaugural address, and charged a conspiracy among Buchanan, Taney, and Douglas. The next decision, warned countless newspapers and speechmakers, would impose slavery upon the states themselves.

The Political Quest for Peace and Votes

Taney's decision coincided unhappily with the final efforts of the Kansas proslavers. Because the Kansas Free-Soilers, who were in the majority, refused to vote either for delegates to a new constitutional convention or on the question of slavery after the constitution was finished, the proslave party was able to present Congress with the ratified proslave LeCompton constitution and ask for statehood under its terms. And for once, James Buchanan made a firm decision. To restore sectional harmony he demanded the immediate admission of Kansas under this constitution.

These combined efforts of Taney, Buchanan, and the Le-Compton Democrats would have ruined a lesser man than Stephen A. Douglas, who was compelled by both expediency and principle to support Taney but to fight Buchanan and the LeCompton constitution. Douglas faced an election campaign in 1858, and the people of Illinois would make no concession to the South beyond popular sovereignty and would tolerate popular sovereignty only so long as it spelled freedom. Beyond 1858, however, lay 1860, and Southerners would never support a presidential candidate who dared repudiate the Dred Scott decision. Reconciling a court decree which denied the right of territorial citizens to prohibit slavery with a doctrine advocating the right of settlers to decide the matter for themselves required considerable imagination, but Douglas had it. The Court's view that any citizen could take slaves to any territory was correct, he announced, but the right would be useless unless local territorial legislatures passed the necessary police regulations for its enforcement. Thus popular sovereignty was still the practical solution.

More pressing, however, was the LeCompton constitution.

The Death of Slavery

"By God, Sir," said Douglas, "I made James Buchanan, and by God, Sir, I will unmake him." With no apparent hesitation, Douglas joined his Republican enemies in the battle against the admission of Kansas with the proslave constitution. The usually placid Buchanan was roused to anger and ordered all loyal Democrats to combine against Douglas. Illinois newspapers supporting Douglas were deprived of government advertising and printing, and local officeholders were ordered to organize public meetings against him.

Other Northern Democrats had also supported popular sovereignty in the faith that it would mean a free Kansas and were fully aware of the danger to themselves if it did not. After many weeks of fierce debate, the Douglas Democrats and Republicans passed a bill which gave Kansas another election, and in August, 1858, the Kansas Territory officially rejected slavery forever.

American politics had a strange new alignment. The Republicans had won Kansas for freedom, but they had lost it as a political issue. Their party needed a new program and new leadership. Stephen A. Douglas had led the fight against the LeCompton constitution and was in the eyes of President Buchanan no longer a Democrat. Perhaps the Little Giant and his sweeping ambitions for the economic development of an expanded America could be recruited for the Republican party. At least Horace Greeley and several other Republican leaders hoped so. Illinois Republicans who had spent years fighting Douglas, however, disagreed.

A house divided against itself cannot stand. I believe this government cannot endure permanently half slave and half free. I do not expect the Union to be dissolved; I do not expect the house to fall; but I do expect it will cease to be divided. It will become all one thing, or all the other. Either the opponents of slavery will arrest the further

pread of it, and place it where the public mind shall rest in the
belief that it is in the course of ultimate extinction, or its advocates
will push it forward till it shall become alike lawful in all the States,
old as well as new, North as well as South.

The speaker was Abraham Lincoln, and his oration was designed to convince Republicans and Free-Soilers everywhere
that Stephen A. Douglas had no place in their ranks. Only a
few hours before, an Illinois Republican convention had re-
buked Horace Greeley and other national leaders for their new
feeling toward Douglas by declaring Lincoln the party's official
candidate for senator against Douglas. In response, Lincoln
argued with occasionally specious facts and logic, but with
magnificent political acumen, that slavery, if unchecked by law,
would take over the free states. Douglas, he continued, had no
moral objections to slavery, and the house divided could become all free only by entrusting the government to leaders who
considered slavery morally wrong and would put it on the road
to ultimate extinction.

The "house divided" image was politically risky and later
cost Lincoln some needed votes, but "ultimate extinction" was
a product of sheer political genius. It could mean tomorrow or
a thousand years hence, depending upon the hearer or reader.

This is not to say that Lincoln was consciously cynical in his
choice of words. He had often expressed a moral revulsion
against slavery, but as a child of the upland South, and, indeed,
of his times, he considered the Negro race inferior, and was
painfully aware of the problems which would accompany the
disappearance of the institution. He had no discernible ambition
to tamper with Southern slavery at the risk of further sectional
conflict, but up until the Kansas-Nebraska act he had apparently found comfort in a faith that at some point in the distant

future some new set of circumstances would permit its peaceful destruction. By his own public testimony, at least, it was the moral indifference implied in popular sovereignty rather than its practical results that had roused Lincoln's ire. All hope for the eventual death of slavery required a continued moral repugnance toward slavery by the public, and the institution's permanent confinement within its present limits. Thus, according to Lincoln, every possibility of slavery expansion, however remote in fact, must be opposed for symbolic as well as practical reasons. Since the anti-Negro sentiments of most westerners as well as the climate and geography of the remaining territories had made popular sovereignty in fact a road to freedom, the moral issue was also essential to Lincoln's political campaign against Douglas. For Lincoln, expediency and principle were identical just as they had been for Douglas when confronted with the LeCompton constitution.

The famous debates which followed gave the Republican party a new national leader and a new program—ultimate extinction to begin with containment. Lincoln, however, insisted vehemently that he had no designs against slavery where it already existed and that he would not oppose the fugitive slave act. Lincoln charged throughout the debates that Douglas had been part of a deliberate conspiracy to nationalize slavery. Douglas answered by citing the active opposition of Buchanan's friends in Illinois, the free status of Kansas, and his own opposition to the LeCompton constitution. In turn the Little Giant used the "house divided" speech to show that Lincoln was promoting sectional conflict over a meaningless question since slavery could expand no further under any circumstances. Douglas shamelessly appealed to racial prejudice. Lincoln accepted the validity of racial supremacy and denied that he had ever advocated or believed in political or social equality for Negroes. There was, however, a strong difference in the tone of the two racial philosophies, however similar, and Lincoln at least contradicted himself occasionally by insisting that all men regardless of race or color should have an equal right to earn a living.

In effect, Douglas argued that slavery could not and would not be extended, while Lincoln insisted that slavery should not and must not be extended. At Freeport, Illinois, Douglas answered Lincoln by restating the doctrine he had already expressed several times before. By virtue of the Dred Scott decision, he reasoned, slaveholders with slaves could not be barred from entering any territory by the federal government. This right, however, would be meaningless if local territorial legislatures refused to enact the police regulations necessary to protect the slaveholder's right to slave property. Thus, said Douglas, regardless of the Court's edict, territorial legislatures could effectively bar slavery during the territorial stage.

Southern leaders would admit no such territorial right before the actual point of application for statehood. Still, before his opposition to the LeCompton constitution, Douglas had stated his Freeport view without significant Southern criticism. Indeed, various Southerners, including Jefferson Davis, had on different occasions stated the same opinion in refuting the charge that they were trying to seize the West for slavery. The Freeport doctrine of 1858 was probably the excuse rather than the reason for the angry storm against Douglas in the South. The real crime of Douglas in Southern eyes was his cooperation with the hated Republicans against the LeCompton constitution.

Douglas won reelection to the Senate, but Lincoln had gained national stature and had given the Republican party the doctrine of ultimate extinction. With magnificent eloquence Lincoln had expressed the highest moral ideals in language which required no sacrifice from anyone. Indeed, Lincoln considered himself and his principles well-calculated to lead America toward sectional peace. If the popular conscience could be soothed by the belief that slavery could not expand, he argued, the antislavery agitation would become unnecessary and would probably cease.

The Southern support Douglas would need for the presidential election of 1860 had been further eroded, but the Little Giant had had no choice. He could not have held his even more important Northern supporters had he spoken any differently. In September, 1859, Douglas wooed the North still further with an article in *Harper's Weekly* which reiterated the Freeport doctrine in only slightly different language. The Southern press again rang with angry denunciations against the only friendly Northern leader who had a chance to keep the hated Republicans from winning the White House in 1860.

XI

The Cold War and John Brown

> The South has acted . . . according to the almost
> universal usage of civilized mankind and the in-
> junctions of the Bible. . . . She flourishes like the
> bay tree, whilst Europe starves, and she is as re-
> markable for her exemption from crime as her
> freedom from poverty. She is by far . . . the most
> prosperous and happy country in the world. Her
> jealous and dependent rivals have begun to imitate
> her. They must soon openly approve her course in
> order to vindicate themselves.
>
> GEORGE FITZHUGH

Those who loved the Union were indeed star-crossed. A brief
but painful commercial depression in 1857, which idled fifty
thousand workers in New York City alone, reflected the usual
American problem of a money and credit system inadequate
for the resources, talents, and dreams of the American people.
The industrial North suffered much; the agrarian South far less.
Earlier in the year, Southern and certain northwestern mem-

bers of Congress had passed a free-trade tariff bill, and Northerners were quick to blame their troubles on this legislation The actual need for tariff protection was less than northeasterners thought, but this further domination of the Congress by the slave power brought more Northern speeches and editorials against slavery. The South responded with the usual hurt feelings and anger. When the hapless Buchanan vetoed another homestead act and announced his opposition to all river and harbor legislation, westerners were again roused to fury against this continued thwarting by the slavocracy of their rights and manifest destiny.

In turn, various Southern papers and leaders actually exulted in the Northern plight and argued that the situation demonstrated clearly the superiority of their own economic system. The times appeared to be uniquely appropriate for the publication of George Fitzhugh's *Cannibals All: or, Slaves without Masters*. In this work of fantasy, Fitzhugh attacked the Northern wage system as cannibalistic and boldly predicted that the North would eventually switch to slavery for the benefit of the workers themselves.

The pride and comfort gained by Southerners from Fitzhugh, however, did not equal the fear and anger roused by Hinton Rowan Helper's *Impending Crisis of the South: How to Meet It*. Helper, a North Carolinian, mixed the humanitarian antislavery arguments of Washington and Jefferson with his own harsh racism, but denounced slavery and slaveholders above all for their domination and exploitation of the vast non-slaveholding white population. The South was ignorant, poor, and backward, said Helper, and would remain so until slavery was abolished and Negroes were colonized elsewhere. Helper's open call for class warfare between rich and poor was answered by ntensified racist propaganda from the slaveholding leaders. If Helper's suggestions were followed, warned Albert G. Brown of Mississippi, the Negro "will insist upon being treated as an equal—that he shall go to the white man's table and the white man to his—that he shall share the white man's bed, and the white man his—that his son shall marry the white man's daughter, and the white man's daughter his son."

In another act of defiance in the face of criticism, various Southern leaders began advocating a reopening of the African slave trade. The long-standing law prescribing the death penalty for slavers had been passed with almost unanimous support of Southerners, including John C. Calhoun, and most Southerners still opposed the trade. A few, however, answered Helper's attempt to rouse antislavery feelings among the poorer whites by arguing that the reopening of the trade would drive down prices until every small farmer could own at least one slave. The arguments probably affected more Northern abolitionists than Southerners and were answered with another barrage of criticism against all things Southern.

A more concrete aspect of the slave trade question was the failure of Southern juries to convict or even indict ship captains and owners virtually taken in the act of smuggling slaves from Africa. In several spectacular cases, usually involving flagrant cruelty toward the human cargo, slavers were released and the courts were justified by Southern arguments equating these actions with Northern refusal to enforce the fugitive slave laws.

Another Southern heretic, Representative Frank Blair of Missouri, a sponsor of Helper's book, asked Congress to acquire territory in Central or South America as a place for colonizing free Negroes and liberated slaves. In an impassioned speech which he repeated often in the years 1857–60 Blair begged

The Death of Slavery

Southerners to recognize the evils of slavery and its inevitable death and take advantage of his proposal. In a burst of double-edged racism, Blair argued that Negro inferiority dictated the removal of all freed slaves to another land, but that an influx of former slaves blessed by association with Anglo-Saxon whites would actually raise the cultural and political level of the Latin American areas where they might be sent. Even those Southerners who managed to read through to the more acceptable parts of Blair's long speeches were only infuriated by his overall message.

The election of Douglas and the emergence of Lincoln were only part of the political story of 1858. Throughout the North the Republicans swept the gubernatorial, state legislative, and congressional elections almost everywhere. There were various possible reasons. Anger against the Dred Scott decision and the encroachments, however imaginary, of the slave power played a role, but the general economic suffering must have been equally important. Northerners could express their dissatisfaction with the depression and the obvious incompetence of Buchanan only by voting for either the Republicans or the Know-Nothings, and the latter clearly had no chance for real power. Southerners, however, saw the election only as further proof of Northern hostility. Southern fire-eaters were encouraged. The election of a Republican President in 1860, they hoped fervently, would be the final proof to the Southern people that only secession and independence could save their honor and safety.

The irritations and name-calling would have practical meaning, however, only if the South resorted to overt action, and until October, 1859, the evidence indicates that the lamentations of radicals like Rhett, Yancey, Ruffin, and others, were falling upon at least half-deaf ears. Southerners who did not really want to emigrate westward with slaves and Southerners who preferred a West without Negroes if they should emigrate, remained unconvinced that the Yankees, however hateful they might be, had any really serious intentions against Southern slavery. Ultimate extinction, after all, when combined with orthodox racial views and promises to obey the Constitution, leave slavery alone, and enforce the fugitive slave act, was not a very threatening doctrine.

Southerners and Northerners who wanted peace, however, had not reckoned with John Brown, late of Osawatomie, Kansas.

Even before his last invasion of Missouri and trip to Canada with the escaped slaves, John Brown, product of a family cursed by insanity and himself a failure in various shady as well as honest wealth-seeking enterprises, had decided that the Lord had still bigger plans for his talents. He would invade Virginia, capture the federal arsenal at Harper's Ferry, call upon Virginia slaves to revolt, arm those closest at hand for the holy conflict, and march southward to coordinate the spontaneous rebellions that would naturally erupt in answer to his invitation. In case the arsenal should disappoint his expectations, he had ordered from a New England blacksmith a thousand sharp metal-pointed hand pikes said to be excellent weapons in hand to hand combat.

Brown later assured a court that he had intended only to repeat the Missouri venture on a larger scale and had intended no violence. His true intentions, however, had been committed to paper as well as outlined to numerous witnesses and supporters. He did not explain the selection of an arsenal for the initial attack, and those who remembered the severed limbs of his Kansas victims needed no explanation for the pikes.

157

The Death of Slavery

Had the Virginia slaves flocked to Brown's banner, Brown might have set the cause of emancipation back another century. With more luck he might have caused the deaths of a great many people of both races and thereby given Northerners a new set of reasons for believing Southern arguments that the Africans must be kept in bondage.

As it was, the expedition caused only a brief moment of excitement, a handful of innocent casualties, and the capture and execution of Brown for treason, murder, and inciting slaves to rebellion. He denied all three charges. "Had I interfered," said Brown, "in behalf of the rich, the powerful, the intelligent, the so-called great . . . or any of that class . . . it would have been all right; and every man in this court would have deemed it an act worthy of reward rather than punishment."

Brown's raid was an isolated affair led by a unique fanatic, and had Southern leaders treated it as such it might have remained a failure. The old man's Northern backers were burning evidence and running for cover in all directions, and imprisonment would have denied him the martyrdom needed for a legend. The erratic and ambitious Governor Henry Wise of Virginia, however, prevented an examination for insanity, and dramatized in every possible way both the conspiracy and his own role in thwarting it. In the face of death, Brown spoke with moving eloquence and behaved with magnificent valor. His last hours gave his life and death a symbolic meaning which enabled many Northerners to forget his past crimes and cruelties. Imaginative writers, including Victor Hugo, were soon rewriting Brown's life to put it all in character with his death. Henry David Thoreau, for example, wrote:

Some eighteen hundred years ago Christ was crucified. This morning, perchance, Captain Brown was hung. These are the two ends of

158

chain which is not without its links. He is not Old Brown any longer; he is an angel of light. I see now that it was necessary that the bravest and humanest man in all the country should be hung. . . I *almost fear* that I may yet hear of his deliverance, doubting if a prolonged life, if *any* life, can do as much good as his death.

As at least one observer noted, it was much easier to put him on a scaffold than to get him off.

Brown's exploit swept Southerners into a state of irrationality from which most of them never recovered. For the first time, the fire-eaters had proof that Calhoun and his successors had been right—that the North really did intend to invade the South and incite the slaves to a bloody revolt. Edmund Ruffin gathered up the pikes for exhibition to his audiences as he traveled around the South on his pilgrimage to rouse people to their danger. Politicians, newspapers, and ministers reminded Southerners of the horrible race war in Haiti half a century earlier. Brown was indeed a godsend to the Southern radicals, and in the end they completed his work. The South ultimately did to itself what the North if unprovoked by a war for disunion might never have done.

Southerners demanded a disavowal of Brown from the North, and at first all but a few ultraradicals criticized him sharply. Poets and essayists like Emerson, Thoreau, Whittier, Bryant, and others, however, saw the deed in another light, and Northern pulpits were soon dedicating hymns to the memory of St. John the Just. However insane and cruel he had been on occasion, Brown had died like a hero for a worthy cause, and his story was a magnet for literary talents seeking a dramatic theme.

Naturally enough, Southerners considered any defense of Brown a wicked attitude shared by the entire North. Southern

The Death of Slavery

voices of reason found the going hard after John Brown. The martyred murderer had struck a nerve in the minds and hearts of the great Southern majority of non-slaveholders who were ready to believe the worst about slave character and succumb to fears often more intense than those of people who actually owned and had contact with the slave population.

XII

Secession

I have no purpose directly or indirectly to interfere with the institution of slavery in the States
where it exists. I believe I have no lawful right to
do so, and I have no inclination to do so.

ABRAHAM LINCOLN, 1858, AND
REPEATED IN FIRST INAUGURAL
ADDRESS

As the fateful year 1860 began, Senator Jefferson Davis set the
tone with a set of resolutions for the consideration of his
colleagues. The federal government, he argued, was obligated
to give slavery all needful protection in the territories. The
people in the territories should have no say on the matter until
the coming of statehood, although even Davis still admitted that
at the moment of statehood any area could decide for itself.

In effect, Davis was insisting upon a federal slave code and
rejecting popular sovereignty and its author. A presidential
election lay just ahead, and since the hated Douglas had taken

a stand which should have been acceptable to any thinking Southerner, Davis and his friends had to approach the limits of absurdity to find a base for their opposition. Douglas more than held his own in the ensuing debates, but the radical Southern press again oversimplified his arguments and turned them into the words of an enemy of the South.

In the harmonious party atmosphere of 1856, the Democrats had awarded the 1860 convention to Charleston, South Carolina. The choice was fatal. Flower-bedecked Charleston in April, with the plantation families, including their beautiful daughters in for the glittering social season, seemed to personify all that was best in the civilization glorified by the Southern ultras. Every local popular pressure played into the hands of the radicals as they methodically set about to destroy the political party they could no longer rule.

Northern Democrats came to Charleston to nominate Stephen A. Douglas and write popular sovereignty into the national platform. William L. Yancey of Alabama, Robert B. Rhett of South Carolina, Edmund Ruffin of Virginia, and their friends had other ideas. They would demand an unattainable plank calling for federal protection of slavery in all territories, and they would bolt the convention and split the party in retaliation for their failure. The inconsistency of simultaneous demands for a federal government too weak to bar slavery but strong enough to impose it upon unwilling territories bothered them not at all. They had already abandoned any real hope of further slave territories within the bounds of the United States, but to the South lay Cuba, Mexico, Central America, and other island areas which might be taken once their natural talents and energies were liberated from restricting Northern influences. They would choose their own candidate, who would be deeated by a black Republican, and the Southern people would then recognize the need for a final separation.

Largely because of his hatred for Douglas, President Buchanan cooperated fully. Democratic officeholders obligated to Buchanan could easily be made to understand that the elevation of Douglas to the leadership of the party would put Democratic unionists in control of the federal patronage. Whether or not, as some have believed, the nomination of Douglas before the platform debate would have changed the result, Old Buck played a major role in blocking this arrangement.

Driven to new heights of blazing oratory by the cheering galleries, Yancey and his friends recited their catalogue of alleged Northern oppressions and Southern wrongs. In the end, however, protection for territorial slavery was voted out and popular sovereignty was voted in. In a great scene of dramatic excitement, the delegations from the Deep South took their cues and marched out, and the Democratic party, America's last great bond of national unity, was torn apart. Within a few weeks, the Northern Democrats had nominated Douglas, while the bolters had turned to Vice-President John Breckinridge of Kentucky.

Somewhat later, a group of former Southern Whigs still unwilling to cooperate with Democrats joined forces with former Northern Whigs averse both to Republican radicalism and to former Democrats turned Free-Soil Republicans. The result was the Constitutional Union party, liberally spiced also with Know Nothings, which nominated John Bell of Tennessee.

The Republicans, meanwhile, had convened in Chicago with their great New York leader, William Henry Seward, as the obvious choice. In February, 1860, Seward countered his

The Death of Slavery

earlier "higher law" and "irrepressible conflict" doctrines with a widely publicized plea for tolerance and sectional harmony. While Seward sincerely disliked slavery, his eloquent anti-slavery speeches had often been a mere pose assumed for the practical purpose of winning elections.

Seward's discovery that the sectional differences were essentially economic rather than moral came too late, however. In the same month, the ungainly but eloquent prairie lawyer Abraham Lincoln delivered a masterly address at Cooper's Union in New York City. With a brilliantly delivered argument documenting the right and the duty of the federal government to restrict territorial slavery, Lincoln stirred the moral sensibilities of his cheering audience. With a sharp repudiation of John Brown and a long list of assurances to the South that the territorial restriction in no way threatened slavery in its present habitat, he demonstrated his good sense and safeness to a Northern audience spreading far beyond his immediate listeners. "Wrong as we think slavery is," said Lincoln, "we can yet afford to let it alone where it is, because that much is due to the necessity arising from its actual presence in the nation." Still, Lincoln concluded, the North must never compromise to the point of admitting the rightness of slavery. The speech was a sensation, and while his words were still echoing in the press, Lincoln repeated them in several more addresses in New England.

When the Republican convention met in May, a throng of Sewardites from New York paraded through the streets of Chicago behind their own brass band—while noisy Lincoln supporters shrewdly grabbed off the gallery seats in the Wigwam. Seward's enemies combined against him, while the more conservative Lincoln, with his strong western support, had almost no enemies. An arrangement with Simon Cameron, which later brought that worthy a cabinet seat and a refuge as ambassador to Russia when accused of graft in office, gave Pennsylvania to Lincoln and started the bandwagon. The unhappy Seward watched the party he had worked so hard to build cast its lot with Abraham Lincoln, ultimate extinction, opposition to the extension of slavery, assurances of protection for Southern slavery and enforcement of the fugitive slave act, and a magnificent Whig economic program of tariffs, banks, internal improvements, homesteads, free immigration, and a railroad to the Pacific. The phrases of the Declaration of Independence extolling universal freedom and equality were omitted until the ancient abolitionist Joshua Giddings sorrowfully conducted a one-man walkout. At the insistence of George W. Curtis and Frank Blair, the words were inserted and Giddings, with his faith restored, again took his seat amid wild cheering.

In the campaign a few radical Republicans emphasized "extinction" rather than "ultimate," but the effort to picture Lincoln's program as a peaceful solution to the sectional quarrel was far more common. Lincoln himself said little, and Bell said almost nothing. Douglas alone took to the stump in every section to extol popular sovereignty, appeal to moderation, and assure the South that he would crush any rebellion and if necessary hang its leaders.

In Montgomery, Alabama, rotten eggs and tomatoes were thrown at Douglas, but he unflinchingly assured his audience that if made President he would send an army against any effort to secede. The Little Giant was convinced that his Southern enemies were planning to seize the government at Washington and proclaim Breckinridge President if Breckinridge should carry all the slave states. To block such a program Douglas made an especially dynamic campaign in the border states. In answer to Douglas, Breckinridge denied emphatically that he was either a disunionist or secessionist.

Southerners had convinced themselves that the election of Lincoln would be both a mortal insult and a clear and present danger. Their long hold on executive offices and patronage would be broken. Republican-appointed officials would pass abolition propaganda through the mails, enforce restrictions against the slave trade, and refuse to prosecute imitators of John Brown. Above all, slavery itself would be contained, and a President dedicated to the notion that slavery was a moral evil would sit in the White House. Abolitionist armies would invade the South, women and children would be murdered and worse in slave revolts, and everything that made life worth living would be gone if Lincoln were elected. The singing of "John Brown's Body" by marching Lincoln supporters in Northern cities probably had a much greater impact upon Lincoln's Southern enemies than upon his Northern adherents. Moderate Republicans like Seward, Blair, Cameron, and even Greeley, tried to reassure the South, but the few radical speeches by men like Schurz and Sumner were the ones Southerners listened for and heard. False rumors of burnings, slave revolts, and abolition conspiracies swept through the South in the wake of the political orators. The constant state of excitement led occasionally to mob violence and to at least one actual lynching of a helpless citizen suspected of abolitionism.

The election results of 1860 proved, if anything, only that most Americans were moderates on the slave question. Nominated by secessionists, but denying any and all such sentiments, Breckinridge carried by a majority only seven of the fifteen slave states. Together Douglas and Bell had a majority in the other eight, and in the fourteen slave states voting by ballot they received 705,000 votes to 570,000 for Breckinridge. With an economic program aimed at almost every group, Lincoln received only 39.9 per cent of the popular vote, although he would have received an electoral majority even if a single candidate had won the remaining 60.1 per cent.

Between them the two factions of Democrats won control of the Senate, and membership of the House was so close that a handful of splinter party representatives held the balance. As long as the Southerners remained in their congressional seats, Lincoln could not have appointed a postmaster without their approval. The authors of the Dred Scott decision still sat on the Supreme Court. Clearly, Southern slavery was in no danger from the administration of Abraham Lincoln. There would be no further expansion of slavery into new territories, but any real hope for this except through possible conquests in the Caribbean or in Central America had already long since disappeared.

In 1861, however, realities were meaningless. The election of Lincoln was a mortal insult and a Northern popular endorsement of attitudes which made Southern endurance of the Union no longer possible. Southern fears, wounded pride, feelings of persecution, twinges of guilt, and general frustration over a changing world they could not control, were all bound into one package and laid at the door of Abraham Lincoln and the Republican party—both of whom were pledged against any interference with Southern slavery.

From the vantage of hindsight, it is remarkable that Southerners concerned with the threat against slavery drew so little assurance from the racist philosophy shared by most Northerners. For decades Southerners had pointed to the Northern mistreatment of free Negroes as proof of the superior humanity of slavery, and the evidence had supported their charges. The contradiction between American idealism and American racism was never more apparent than in 1860. In every Northern state Negroes were victims of outrageous discrimination and segregation, whether in education, economic opportunity, public services, politics, or courts of justice. Jim Crow was in full swing in stagecoaches, steamships, and railroads. Indeed, Southern slaveholders traveling through Northern states could keep slaves with them in cars which excluded local free Negro citizens. Efforts to start Negro schools had usually yielded to implacable white resistance even in parts of New England. Negroes voted in only five states, which included only 6 per cent of the Northern Negro population. Even where legal suffrage existed, other qualifications and personal intimidation kept many from the polls.

The Free-Soil movement itself had been strongly spiced with racism. Many of its leaders wanted neither slaves nor free Negroes in the western territories, and excluding the former in the present was well-calculated to preserve the absence of the latter in the future. In 1848 the few Negro voters had given but little support to the Free Soil party because of the racial implications in many of its arguments. In many cases, the prejudice which motivated the Free-Soiler made him equally ready to oppose the abolition of slavery in the South.

Too many Southerners, however, saw Free-Soilers, abolitionists, Republicans, and Yankees in general, as self-righteous enemies no longer to be tolerated. Avery Craven has suggested that the key to Southern behavior in 1861 was the Southerners' dread of being pushed into the modern world. Others have answered that the South in fact had already accepted the modern world—its ideology as well as its technology—and that

Secession

their awareness, however subconscious, of the true nature of slavery when placed in this context, created inner conflicts in the Southern mind which made rational behavior impossible. The difference in these views is more apparent than real. For Southerners, the preservation of slavery in the kind of America that plainly lay ahead would mean the continuation of life under a smothering cloud of moral condemnation which no one under existing circumstances could prove false. Most people love those who increase their self-esteem and hate those who inspire the discomfort of moral self-doubt. Southern secessionists in 1861 were no exception. They would free themselves forever from the plague of incessant Northern reproach. Their newly created independent nation would then by its prosperity, happiness, power, and cultural achievements, demonstrate the glories of slavery and the wicked falsehoods of their tormentors. Secession had become a desperate emotional need for people who saw it as the only hope for guiding their future into paths that would justify their past and vindicate their present. If the Yankees resisted the secession, the Southerners would prove their superiority immediately. For many Southerners, the chance to strike a physical blow at the hated enemy had an appeal strong enough by itself to generate a civil war.

Assured by Lincoln and Douglas alike that Southern slavery was safe, but warned by both that secession would not be tolerated, seven states of the deep South seceded in rapid succession. By February, 1861, they had formed the Confederate States of America with a new national constitution and federal government seated in Montgomery, Alabama.

With his usual firmness, President Buchanan announced that states had no right to secede, but that the federal government had no right to coerce them if they did.

The Congress made frantic efforts to find a formula which

would bring back the errant sisters. The aged John J. Crittenden of Kentucky, with one son destined to be a Union major general while another held the same rank for the Confederacy, offered an amendment to extend the Missouri Compromise line to the Pacific. Exhausted and ill, the indomitable Douglas proposed popular sovereignty for all territories, with the slavery decision to be made when the population reached 50,000. The Secretary of State-to-be and former apostle of the "higher law," William H. Seward, suggested an amendment which would leave the territorial issue untouched, deprive Congress forever of any power to touch slavery where it existed, give all fugitive slaves a trial by jury, and repeal all Northern laws designed to help fugitive slaves. All such efforts failed to pass. With seven states missing, those who would make concessions to the South were in the minority. For most Republicans the secession was merely a form of blackmail which if successful in getting concessions would lead only to greater future demands and might even encourage other states to secede.

Various historians both Northern and Southern have criticized the President-elect for not supporting the suggested compromises. Numerous leaders pleaded for his help, but after much painful vacillation Lincoln refused to intervene. He was apparently ready to compromise on almost any question except his party's stand against the further extension of slavery. The Crittenden proposal would give slavery at least a chance, however small, in the areas south of 36° 30′, and Seward's amendment would have created a constitutional barrier against ultimate extinction. In his first inaugural address Lincoln repeated his earlier pledges that Southern slavery would remain inviolate and that the fugitive slave laws would be enforced to the best of his ability. He was not prepared, however, to abandon the basic Free-Soil position upon which his party had been built. He was a flexible politician in the best sense of the word, but a reversal of his earlier stand against territorial slavery would have required too great a sacrifice of personal integrity.

The sacrifice, furthermore, would have been wasted on the seceded states. The compromise efforts were important to relations between the administration and the border slave states, but none of Lincoln's historian critics have offered any evidence that the seceded states would have returned in 1861 on any basis whatever. The minimum acceptable concession would have been an official endorsement of all the alleged superior moral advantages of slavery, and even this would probably have been treated as too little and too late. Since no rational justification for secession existed in the first place, it is difficult to believe that any offer within the power of the President or Congress would have been accepted. The secession leaders had waited too long for the opportunity to try their wings to abandon their victory at the moment of its attainment, and a majority of the Southern people had apparently been captured by the same heady spirit.

In February, 1861, a desperate peace convention of 133 delegates from twenty-one states offered Congress an amendment providing that neither Congress by law nor the nation as a whole by amendment could ever interfere with slavery in any state. The amendment passed the House of Representatives by a two-to-one margin and was quickly ratified by Ohio. Other Northern states appeared ready to follow suit, and it was hoped that some of the seceded states might return for their chance to vote for this guarantee. No such response occurred.

Having denied the right of the South to secede, President Lincoln faced only two alternatives: an unlikely voluntary return by the errant sisters or a restoration of the Union by coercion. A successful coercion might require no more than a show of force on the scale of that threatened by Andrew Jackson in 1833. It might also, however, lead to a major war. To do nothing would avoid trouble for the time being. This would either make the Confederacy stronger or give its members time to feel the disadvantages of being out of the Union. It might eventually bring them back without war. It might also establish the Confederacy as a permanent new nation. Attacking the Confederacy would probably lead other Southern states to secede, and might find only a lukewarm support in the North. Allowing the Confederacy to drive the federal government from its forts and other possessions in the South might have the same effect by demonstrating the strength of the new nation. The federal forts at Pensacola, Florida, and Charleston, South Carolina, would have to be abandoned or defended, and the decision could not be postponed for long.

Like most American Presidents in times of crisis, Abraham Lincoln had to choose from several dangerous alternatives, none of which offered a clearly predictable result. He could not escape the responsibility, he could not improve the quality of his choices, and he had none of the advantages of hindsight.

Secretary of State Seward, whose long-abandoned "higher law" had since been replaced by a willingness to appease the South in almost any way that would restore the Union, promised the border state men the forts would be surrendered. At first, most of the cabinet as well as the ancient General Winfield Scott, still head of the army, agreed with this policy. The equally ancient Francis P. Blair, however, thought differently. Blair had been at the side of Andrew Jackson in 1833 when Old Hickory had crushed the nullification effort of South Carolina. Weakness and appeasement, argued Blair, would mean the permanent division of the Union. Firmness and a show of strength would discourage the seceders and save the Union without war.

On April Fool's Day, 1861, the frantic Seward presented Lincoln with a memorandum suggesting that a quarrel or conflict with another nation might restore the American family circle. Specifically, he proposed demands against Britain, Russia, Spain, and France. Whether or not Lincoln smiled was not recorded. By this time a majority of the cabinet had swung to the side of reinforcing Fort Sumter.

As was his custom, Lincoln listened to everyone, delayed his decision long enough to allow each side to believe it had won the argument, and then sent reinforcements to Fort Sumter under circumstances which have caused historians to disagree ever since. He did not deliberately choose war, but he elected to risk war rather than abandon the symbol of national power in South Carolina.

The confusion which marked the final steps to war was natural enough in the atmosphere of doubt and uncertainty existing everywhere—in Montgomery and Charleston as well as in Washington. After one Lincoln agent had led the Charleston authorities to believe that Fort Sumter would be evacuated, and after Seward had made similar private assurances to various Southerners, the Governor of South Carolina was officially informed that provisions only would be sent to the fort. Resistance to the provisioning, however, Lincoln warned, would result in the use of arms and men.

Jefferson Davis, meanwhile, was being pressured by those convinced that an attack on Sumter would bring seven more slaveholding states, including Virginia and, it was hoped, Maryland, into the Confederacy. Thus Davis saw monumental possibilities in war, while Lincoln saw irretrievable national catastrophe as the likely alternative to war. Neither had any real conception of the magnitude and horror of the war both were contemplating.

The Death of Slavery

The initial plan, proposed by Assistant Navy Secretary Gustavus Fox, called for protection of the expedition by the heavily armed warship *Powhatan*. It was thought that the threat of bombardment by the *Powhatan* would keep the Charleston guns silent and insure a peaceful reinforcement. At the crucial moment, however, Lieutenant David Porter appeared at the Brooklyn Navy Yard with written orders from Lincoln to replace the commander and sail the *Powhatan* to Fort Pickens in Florida. Navy Secretary Welles knew nothing of this, and when informed of it, he angrily led Seward to the White House in the middle of the night and demanded an explanation. The President denied sending the new orders, but Seward showed copies clearly signed by Lincoln. Seward had apparently placed the orders among routine papers where they would be signed without proper consideration. Lincoln ordered Seward to put the *Powhatan* back on its original schedule and destination. Seward wired the correct dispatches to Porter, but signed them with his own name. Porter, already under orders signed by Lincoln superseding those of Welles, chose to ignore new orders signed by a mere Secretary of State. The relief expedition, therefore, sailed without the protection designed to intimidate the Carolinians into peaceful acquiescence. The President calmly ignored Seward's obviously deliberate mistake.

A few minutes before dawn on April 12, 1861, the ancient fire-eater, Edmund Ruffin of Virginia, pulled a lanyard, a mortar fired, and the American Civil War began. The relief ships remained outside the harbor and took no part in the action. The visiting Ruffin, honored with the first shot after his years of agitation, was destined also to fire one of the last. Four years later, when Lee surrendered, Ruffin fired a bullet into his own head.

XIII

War

Clemency on the lips of an American Senator to the malignant enemy of the Republic is cruelty to its friends.

JUSTIN MORRILL

With malice toward none; with charity for all; with firmness in the right, as God gives us to see the right, let us . . . bind up the nation's wounds.

ABRAHAM LINCOLN

The war of American against American and occasionally even brother against brother has inspired millions of written words. It produced more than its share of heroism, dramatic excitement, romance, and incredible endurance. It also killed more young Americans than all other American wars combined.

For the ordinary soldiers and those who prayed for their return, the adventure was little enough compensation for the sacrifices. Homesickness, boredom, and perpetual discomfort, spiced only occasionally with the fear and excitement of battle, was the common lot. In a world without inoculation, sterilization, or wonder drugs, disease and accident took far more lives than the actual battles, even though the fighting has rarely been surpassed for savagery when the troops actually made contact. The Rebel yells and Yankee hurrahs which punctuated the beginnings of battle all too quickly gave way to the silence of the dead and the screams and groans of the wounded. Steel-tired, horse-drawn ambulances piled high with sufferers lurched along trackless battlefields and rut-filled roads to primitive hospitals where ill-trained surgeons, unaware that germs existed, operated and amputated without benefit of adequate anesthesia or clean instruments. Typhoid, infection, gangrene, and tetanus played no favorites between North and South.

While blessed with tremendous advantages in population, wealth, and technology, the North was plagued with inadequate military leadership and political disunity. Outmanned and out-gunned, but never outfought, the South enjoyed certain advantages which prolonged the otherwise unequal contest until vast areas had been laid waste and more than 600,000 men had died. For the South, anything less than unconditional surrender would be a victory. Its soldiers fought on their own soil and defended their homes, families, property, and institutions against the Yankee invaders. It was a simple cause which even the least imaginative could understand. Conversely, the Union soldier was fighting for an abstract ideal—the preservation of a nation state. The catchwords Union, freedom, and democracy were inspiring, but the reasons why they could not be properly enjoyed without the presence of the unwilling Southern states were not always clear. Although the Emancipation Proclamation kept millions of ordinary Europeans, if not their leaders, on the side of the North, there is no evidence that it provided any significant inspiration to many of the Northern soldiers. Indeed, the legislature of the President's home state of Illinois criticized Lincoln sharply for this action.

The new Southern nation suffered from incessant quarreling among its political leaders, as Jefferson Davis proved incapable of unifying states that were just as defiant of his authority as they had been of that in Washington. The Confederacy, however, did have some of the most talented military leaders ever seen on a battlefield, and even the sporadic interference of President Davis could not keep Robert E. Lee from taking almost every possible advantage of Northern misjudgment, mismanagement, and timidity.

Success or failure for the military man depends in large part upon the quality of his opposition, and throughout most of the war, the iron-nerved Virginian Lee was singularly blessed by the frequent hesitation and sheer incompetence of the generals assigned the task of defeating him. Five different commanding generals, each with overwhelming superiority in manpower and arms, tried unsuccessfully to lead or drive an army the mere 110 miles separating Washington from the Confederate capital at Richmond.

In July, 1861, at Bull Run in northern Virginia, General Irvin McDowell's army was turned back by the Confederates under Pierre G. T. Beauregard. Stonewall Jackson made his immortal stand, Senator Ben Wade joined the battle, the city of Washington became hysterical over the possibility of an invasion, and the Confederates were as confused by victory as the Northerners were by defeat.

During the following spring, General George McClellan ferried an enormous army down the Chesapeake and up the

York River to a point just east of Richmond. Meanwhile, however, a small force under Stonewall Jackson advanced on Washington and frightened Secretary of War Stanton into recalling the army of McDowell from its original assignment to reinforce McClellan. With overwhelming superiority and only 4½ miles from Richmond, McClellan delayed until Jackson had time to rejoin Lee. Fortified with information from his great cavalry commander, J. E. B. Stuart, who had ridden entirely around the Union army, Lee attacked. The ensuing Seven Days' Battles ended with a Union retreat of 20 miles back to the protection of gunboats on the James River. McClellan was still in an excellent position for renewing the attack but Lincoln was persuaded by General Henry Halleck and McClellan's congressional enemies to withdraw the army and combine it with another already commanded by the boastful and incompetent General John Pope.

On August 30, the armies met again at Bull Run. Through Pope's mistakes, a great Union army was again thoroughly routed by the skill of General Lee.

Inspired by this victory, Lee crossed the Potomac into Maryland, and McClellan, by now restored to command, gave chase. On September 13, a Union soldier found three cigars wrapped with a copy of Lee's "Special Orders No. 191," indicating that a considerable part of the Confederate army had been sent elsewhere. Even with this information, McClellan delayed his attack until Lee had assumed a strong position on Antietam Creek. The battle drove Lee back into Virginia, but McClellan missed a magnificent opportunity for effective pursuit. Three weeks later, Stuart again rode round McClellan's army. "When I was a boy," said Abraham Lincoln, "we used to play a game called 'Three times round and out.' Stuart has

been round McClellan twice. The third time McClellan will
be out."

Before the third time, however, McClellan was replaced by
General Ambrose Burnside, whose long side whiskers gave the
English language a new word. Burnside protested his inad-
equacy and quickly proved it at Fredericksburg with several
rash frontal assaults against Lee's impregnable hilltop fortifica-
tions. "It is well that war is so terrible," said Lee as he watched
the frightful slaughter, "or we should grow too fond of it."

Burnside was replaced by another congressional favorite,
Fighting Joe Hooker. With a rash of bombastic slogans and
exhortations, Hooker marched 130,000 men southward to face
Lee's 62,000 at Chancellorsville. A brilliant maneuver by
Stonewall Jackson threw the Union command into confusion,
and in the midst of the battle a falling pillar struck Hooker on
the head. Before losing consciousness he ordered a general
retreat. The ensuing rout and slaughter was an expensive
Southern victory, however, because at its end the irreplaceable
Stonewall Jackson lay mortally wounded.

Again Lee struck out for a victory in the North in the hope
that it would cause an effective popular demand for the Yankees
to abandon the struggle. At Gettysburg, Pennsylvania, on July
1, 1863, Lee faced superior Union forces commanded now by
General George G. Meade. Meade fought a skillful defensive
battle, and after the heroic but futile charge of 15,000 Confederates under General George E. Pickett had failed, Lee was
compelled to retreat with a badly shattered army.

Meade had won the greatest Union victory of the war, but
he was unpopular with Congress. His failure to pursue Lee
soon brought another change in command, but this time
Lincoln had found his man of the hour. A seedy-looking little

man with a decidedly unmilitary bearing stepped off a train in Washington—Ulysses S. Grant had come to change the style of the war.

Happily for the North, during the long, dreary months of failure, the Union navy had blockaded the Southern coastline with enough success to cause significant shortages and genuine hardship. In April, 1861, Commander Samuel Phillips Lee, U.S.N., cousin of Robert E. Lee, was en route to the Far East when he learned of the attack on Fort Sumter. Ignoring previous orders, he turned his ship around and raced home for service to the Union. A few months later, he devised a new and extremely effective blockading technique whereby ships were carefully dispersed according to speed and firepower. Since the system of awarding the spoils of naval battle to the victorious officers and crews was still in effect during the Civil War, the Yankee Lee made more money from the war than any other military figure. He later used much of it for the rehabilitation of his Southern relatives.

As part of the blockading process, Union ships captured bases and forts up and down the Atlantic. Officers like Samuel F. DuPont, Melancton Smith, John Dahlgren, and the spectacular David Porter performed heroically. Blockade runners occasionally got through, but the Union navy captured or destroyed 295 steamers and nearly 1,100 sailing vessels and rowboats. Forty of the captured steamers were converted to Union blockaders.

Southern naval achievements, except those of the British-built cruisers *Alabama* and *Florida*, were more exciting than significant. The armored *Merrimac* fought the little round-turreted *Monitor* in the first battle of ironclads. The world's first sinking by a submarine occurred when the 35-foot Confederate *R. L. Hunley* rammed the USS *Housatonic* with its single torpedo. Both ships were destroyed.

Under Captains Raphael Semmes and J. N. Maffit, the *Alabama* and *Florida* terrorized Northern shipping for months, but eventually the *Alabama* was sunk and the *Florida* was captured and "accidentally" sunk.

The help expected by the South from Europe did not materialize. The loss of Southern cotton caused some hardship in Britain, but substantial shipments of Northern wheat—some of it financed by American philanthropy—helped feed the British masses. The aristocratic Southern slaveholding society contradicted the ideals which represented the aspirations of working people everywhere, and British and French working people were therefore instinctively pro-Union. The ruling classes in both nations were emotionally identified with the South, and those concerned with national power saw the division of the Union as the weakening of a rival.

In England, the brilliant American ambassador, Charles Francis Adams, and his equally able son, Henry, did a masterful job of reminding the British government of the rules of neutrality and keeping the working masses sympathetic to the Union. Henry Adams, in particular, delivered speeches and campaigned for sympathy with the Union at numerous labor meetings. Perhaps equally important, British leaders decided that the precedents being set by the bold acts of Union blockaders would come in handy in some future war when the British navy might wish to take the same steps against American or other ships seeking to trade with the European continent. In 1914–15 the British would invoke vivid memories of the American Civil War.

The Death of Slavery

The most serious crisis with Britain occurred when the brash American Captain Charles Wilkes stopped a British ship on the high seas and abducted the Confederate agents, Mason and Slidell. Wilkes became a national hero overnight, but Lincoln accepted the advice of Seward, Sumner, and others, defied public opinion, and freed the envoys. By every standard of international law, the British protests were justified, and the captives were not worth the ill-feelings being stirred up by the incident.

A British private firm, however, built the powerful *Alabama* and *Florida* for the Confederacy, and official carelessness allowed them to escape. The still more powerful Laird rams were also built, but the vigilance and strong arguments of Adams kept them confined to the shipyards.

Meanwhile, the naval war on the Gulf of Mexico and the rivers was equally important. Admiral Farragut's fleet rammed through the Southern barricades, ships, and shore batteries to open the Mississippi and take New Orleans, and Union gunboats performed brilliantly on the Tennessee and Cumberland Rivers. "Damn the torpedoes, full speed ahead!" shouted Farragut, as his ships stormed the harbor at Mobile, Alabama, in the greatest naval battle of the war.

In the western theater of action, a new leader had risen from obscurity through solid planning and accomplishment. Ulysses S. Grant had been an ineffective and unhappy student at West Point and after the Mexican War an even unhappier peacetime soldier. Ultimately he had left the army to avoid a court-martial for habitual drunkenness. He had failed at various businesses and jobs when the Civil War suddenly gave him another chance for military fame. His clerk's salary was $50 a month when his

182

West Point background gained him a militia colonelcy. The recommendation of a congressman soon raised him to brigadier general. "You're a general now," said Grant's elderly father. "It's a good job. Don't lose it."

Soon Grant led successful attacks against Fort Henry and Fort Donelson and thereby opened up the Tennessee and Cumberland Rivers for Union transportation into the heart of the South. After a near-defeat at Shiloh in Tennessee, Grant conceived and executed his masterpiece of the war. With magnificent stubbornness and endurance, he led an army through impossible terrain to a position where the all-important Mississippi River city of Vicksburg could be attacked and besieged. On July 4, 1863, as Lee was escaping from Gettysburg, the people of Vicksburg, after long weeks of eating mules and an occasional cat, surrendered to Grant.

After Vicksburg, the Union army moved through Tennessee. At Chickamauga the Confederates under General Bragg severely defeated the forces of General Rosecrans, despite the efforts of General George Thomas. Thomas was a slaveholding Virginian who fought with consistent brilliance for the Union despite the suspicions and criticisms of a Congress unwilling to forgive his background. Chickamauga was soon redeemed at Chattanooga, where the Federals under Thomas and Grant himself successfully stormed Missionary Ridge and Lookout Mountain. The Confederates were thrown back into Georgia, and Tennessee was henceforth Union territory.

Summoned to Washington, Grant took command of the final drive against Richmond, as General Sherman moved through Tennessee and on to Atlanta. After Jefferson Davis insisted upon a Southern stand, and its failure had left Atlanta undefended, Sherman took the city, ordered his men to live off the land, and began his frightfully destructive march across Georgia to the sea. Grant, meanwhile, calmly replaced his ever-mounting casualties, ignored the attacks of Congress, rejected any idea of retreat, and slowly but surely eroded the strength of a magnificently led Southern army that had no replacements. Grant lost 50,000 men in one month, but there were many more available.

As Sherman destroyed Georgia, General Philip Sheridan performed the same service for the Shenandoah valley. The Southern armies were left without food or supplies.

The inevitable day finally arrived when an impeccably dressed Lee rode up to Grant's headquarters at Appomattox Court House. Before accepting the surrender, Grant delayed long enough to correct the more flagrant deficiencies in his always careless attire. It was Grant's finest moment. With great magnanimity he allowed the Southern troops to keep their sidearms and horses, and advised them to go in peace.

It was a tearful farewell when General Lee bade his soldiers good-bye. Before Fort Sumter's fall, Lincoln had offered the Northern command to Lee. The war would have been infinitely cheaper and shorter if the General had loved Virginia less.

Indeed, the outcome of the Civil War was not guaranteed by the obvious Northern superiority. A lesser man in the White House might well have lost the struggle. Abraham Lincoln, however, was astonishingly well-equipped for the challenge thrust upon him. He was a masterful politician with flexible principles and a superb sense of timing. He enjoyed the exercise of responsibility and power. Despite his protestations of humility, which were genuine enough when the President considered his own place in the cosmos, Lincoln in dealing with day-to-day affairs had a superb self-confidence which made him almost impervious to both popular and political pressures in conflict with his own judgment. Lincoln consulted his cabinet and other advisers frequently, but the decisions were his own. He appointed, promoted, demoted, discharged, forgave, punished, submitted, defied, condemned, pardoned, acted, and refused to act—all at his own speed when he thought the time was right. His judgments were not always infallible, but history has judged that they were correct far oftener than not. His mournful countenance symbolized the sufferings of his people. His refusal, indeed his inability, to hate the enemy personally set an example which might have made the postwar story quite different but for the tragedy of his murder, which fanned the very bitterness he had sought to quench.

To keep fighting the war after the initial defeats and disappointments, Northerners had to believe in the eternal value of an undivided Union, and in his ability to expound this faith lies Lincoln's primary claim to greatness. The dead at Gettysburg, said Lincoln in 1863, had died so that the great American experiment in government of, by, and for the people would not fail and thereby betray the lovers of freedom throughout the world. It was a noble concept, but despite the American receptivity to it, it could have been kept alive only by one who believed in it as the only valid justification for the drama of suffering and death in which he found himself a principal actor. "I claim not to have controlled events but confess plainly that events have controlled me," said Lincoln shortly before his assassination. The statement was entirely too modest. With a lesser President, the events which determined the future of the American nation might have been quite different.

While the President's role was that of the prophet who led by idealistic inspiration, the Congress helped build the spirit of hatred, vindictiveness, and sheer competition, which in any war assumes a power all its own after the initial battles. A few congressional leaders continued to hope that after a few skirmishes the Union could be restored in its original form, but radical senators like Wade, Sumner, and Chandler, and representatives like Stevens had no such illusions. The South by its own action had become an independent nation at war with the Union, and realistic Northerners could only fight on that basis or abandon the struggle. The South had achieved a de facto belligerent status from both Queen Victoria's neutrality proclamation and Lincoln's announcement of a blockade. Stevens insisted correctly that Southerners must stand convicted of treason or accept the status of foreign belligerents. To those who argued for Southern constitutional rights, Stevens replied that constitutional obligations repudiated by one party could not be binding upon the other: "When parties become belligerent the war between them abrogates all compacts, treaties, and constitutions . . . between them before the war commenced." To Stevens and his followers, constitutional arguments over such matters as the confiscation acts and the creation of West Virginia were a foolish waste of time. The policies would weaken the rebellion, and this was enough.

In December, 1861, Congress created a radical-dominated Joint Committee on the Conduct of the War, which almost continuously "investigated" until the end of the war. Its eight volumes of hearings, which have been most ably dissected by T. Harry Williams, are a mass of false and contradictory testimony, false interpretations of true evidence, character assassinations of the able and honorable, eulogies for the incompetent and unworthy, and incorrect analyses and views which often did harm to the Union cause.

The committee, however, was a useful fountainhead for the

spirit of war. It inspired constant rumors and charges of treason and conspiracy, and it publicized many alleged Southern atrocities. Most of these had never happened, but in wartime such accounts were far easier to believe than to deny. Some historians have also defended the committee because it occasionally uncovered corruption and waste, it helped keep at least some people on a sharper alert, and it worked constantly for the abolition of slavery. On balance, however, the committee's constructive work was more than offset by sins easily recognizable by students of similar phenomena in the twentieth century.

The radical assumption that any defeat suffered by a Democratic or a non-abolitionist general was clear-cut evidence of treachery and treason led to actions little short of criminal. The Bluff Ben Wade who climbed out of a carriage to join the battle of Bull Run in person commands respect. The Wade who conducted the inquisition of General Charles Stone provokes a very different feeling. Stone faced great odds at Ball's Bluff, and in the battle a former senator turned colonel was killed through his own recklessness. In the emotional wake of this tragedy, General Stone spent fifty days in solitary confinement and a total of 189 days in prison. True, his wife had Southern relatives, he had returned runaway slaves in accord with the law, and, unknown to himself, a Negro refugee had charged him with being friendly to secessionists, but none of this was mentioned at his hearing. The failure to charge him formally or hold a military trial violated the rules of war, and Lincoln was surprisingly negligent. "Why did you not give us these explanations when you were here before?" asked Wade when the general appeared for a final vindication. Stone was restored to rank, but his usefulness was ended.

The Death of Slavery

The committee hounded numerous able generals into oblivion. It encouraged subordinates to disparage and betray their superiors, and found scapegoats for the incompetents who were its favorites. It elevated or helped to elevate Frémont, Pope, and Hooker, and exonerated each of them, as well as General Burnside, of the most appalling incompetence. Stonewall Jackson moved at will through the area defended by Frémont and was thereby able to frighten the administration into recalling the reinforcements with which McClellan might have taken Richmond in June, 1862. Pope, Burnside, and Hooker suffered terrible defeats at the hands of greatly inferior numbers. The committee deprecated General Meade's victory at Gettysburg and plagued him constantly. When Grant stood by Meade and relieved the abolitionist General Butler for the latter's ridiculous performance at Fort Fisher, the committee also turned on Grant. Happily for the Union, Lincoln withstood the pressures until the victories of Grant and Sherman overcame the public dismay over Grant's enormous casualty lists.

The committee thrived on the failures of General McClellan, whose great organizational ability was neutralized by an aversion to large-scale homicide. The General was a West Pointer and a Democrat, he opposed abolition, and he was unable to do the things his Southern counterparts were doing with a fraction of his manpower and material. Profoundly suspicious of all West Pointers, Democrats, and appeasers of slavery, the committee and its Republican followers concluded that only treachery could explain McClellan's failures. From the premise that McClellan did not wish to win the war, the committee moved easily to the next step of persecuting other officers associated with "Little Mac." Ironically, McClellan may have retained his command longer because of the congressional attacks upon him. He became a symbol of the right of the President as Commander-in-Chief to select his own generals, and Abraham Lincoln was a stubborn defender of the American presidency as well as the Union.

The logic of war and the need to give the British and French common people an ideological argument against any assistance by their governments to the South gave the abolitionists their final victory. Slavery had caused the war, and for this reason alone even the most racist Northerner found its defense difficult. More immediately important, slavery was a mainstay of the Southern war effort. Slaves at work meant increased white manpower at the front. The outpouring of radical speeches and committee reports in Congress gave abolition a new orthodoxy as a weapon against the hated Southerners and thereby prepared the Northern mind for an emancipation that few wanted or expected before the war began. Slavery could be defended by no one in the face of the ever-mounting casualty and hospital lists.

"The occasion," said Thaddeus Stevens, "is forced upon us and the invitation presented to strike the chains from four millions of human beings and create them men; to extinguish slavery on this whole continent; to wipe out so far as we are concerned the most hateful and infernal blot that ever disgraced the escutcheon of man; to write a page in the history of the world whose brightness shall eclipse all the records of heroes and sages."

"The rebellion," echoed Charles Sumner, "is slavery itself—incarnate, living, acting, raging, robbing, murdering, according to the essential law of its being."

By the time of Lincoln's proclamation, the Congress had

already gone beyond it. In August, 1861, Congress authorized the seizure of all property used for insurrectionary purposes. This meant slaves digging trenches, building forts, or performing in any way against the United States. In 1862 a second confiscation act prescribed death, fine, or imprisonment for those guilty of treason, and fines, imprisonment, and liberation of their slaves for all "concerned in rebellion or insurrection." In the spring and summer of 1862, Congress authorized voluntary compensated emancipation, abolished slavery in the District of Columbia, ratified a new treaty with Britain for suppression of the African slave trade, abolished slavery without compensation in all territories, forbade the return of any escaped slaves, and declared all such slaves to be free.

At the White House, however, Abraham Lincoln saw other problems and refused to be stampeded into glory. He continued to give serious attention to the arguments of the Blairs that an effective system of colonization must be developed first. He carefully refrained from giving offense to the still loyal border slave states. He promptly revoked the 1861 emancipation decree in Missouri of his western commander, General Frémont, as well as a similar effort in 1862 by General Hunter in Georgia, Florida, and South Carolina. To the impatient Horace Greeley he wrote a public letter describing the question of slavery as entirely secondary to the problem of saving the Union. In messages to Congress in 1861, 1862, and 1863 Lincoln stated his preference for gradual, voluntary, and compensated emancipation, as well as his hope for colonization. In December, 1862, he proposed a program for emancipation within thirty-seven years. The immortal Emancipation Proclamation, designed to strengthen the pro-North spirit of the British and French peoples, took effect on January 1, 1863. It carefully exempted from its provisions the border states and all Confederate slave areas regained by Union troops. Since the second Confiscation Act had contained no exemptions, the Proclamation was in fact a retrogression. It did, however, announce to the world that American slavery had received its mortal wound.

Lincoln's delaying tactics probably strengthened the total war effort, but the angry impatience of the radicals and their later resentment of his deification as the "Great Emancipator" were natural enough. If their fears that peace might come before emancipation were groundless, the President had done nothing to allay them. In fact a Southern surrender in 1861 or even 1862 might have left the cause of abolition in a precarious state. Campaigning against emancipation in 1862, the Democrats made sweeping gains in the Northwest. A century later, the views of Northern white voters on questions involving the completion of the emancipation would still be a question for aspiring politicians, although happily the expected "backlash" of 1964 turned out to be the snap of a wet towel rather than the crack of a whip.

No amount of wishful thinking can obscure the unhappy fact that the racism which underlay the irrational Southern insistence upon secession and war had almost equally deep roots in the North. Americans paid a fearful price for racism in 1861–65, and many decades later there would be the danger of a new price in lost allies and new enemies in Asia, Africa, and Latin America. Not until the excesses of Adolph Hitler and the pressures of the cold war would thoughtful Americans finally mount a serious attack against pseudo-scientific and philosophical bases of racism, and begin practical action to counter its tragic injustices and cruelties.

Eight months ago the African race in this City were literally hunted down like wild beasts. They fled for their lives. When caught, they were shot down in cold blood, or stoned to death, or hung to the

The Death of Slavery

trees or the lamp posts. Their homes were pillaged; the asylum which Christian charity had provided for their orphaned children was burned; and there was no limit to the persecution, but in the physical impossibility of finding further material on which the mob could wreak its ruthless hate. . . .

How astonishing has all this been changed. The same men who could not have shown themselves in the most obscure street in the City without peril of instant death . . . now march in solid platoons, with shouldered muskets, slung knapsacks, and buckled cartridge boxes . . . to the pealing strains of martial music . . . and we are presented with a gorgeous stand of colors in the names of a large number of the first ladies of the City, who attest on parchment . . . that they "will anxiously watch your career, glorying in your heroism, ministering to you when wounded and ill, and honoring your martyrdom with benedictions and with tears." (*New York Times*, March 7, 1864, quoted by Dudley T. Cornish in *The Sable Arm*.)

The participation of Negro soldiers in the Civil War was highly significant. For many months, the President and most of his cabinet resisted the idea, but a few Yankee officers, finding themselves in circumstances which made such action expedient, began the process long before it finally became legal in late 1862. In the beginning the Negro soldiers were used primarily for various laboring tasks, but ultimately they received arms and the usual military training. Many fought chiefly with pick and shovel or saw only limited action as guards behind the lines. Many others, however, took part in some of the bloodiest battles of the war and earned excellent reputations for ability as well as courage. They served in Louisiana, Kansas, Missouri, Arkansas, and up and down the Atlantic coast. They were slaughtered by Forest's raiders at Fort Pillow, Tennessee, and as a result their comrades fought with greater ferocity in subsequent battles. In the Wilderness campaign and at Petersburg they fought heroically, even though, like their white fellows, they were victims of appalling leadership in the catastrophe at

Petersburg. There, many were trapped and slaughtered in the crater resulting after the Union forces had set off a mine under part of the Confederate army. In the final months of the war, they were the entire Twenty-fifth Corps of Grant's army.

The Confederacy, meanwhile, did not enroll Negro soldiers until March, 1865, when the war was already lost. Individual states, however, recruited both slaves and free Negroes throughout the war. The process was usually one of conscription and the soldiers thus acquired were restricted to heavy labor. On rare occasions, a few actually engaged in serious fighting, and many slaves remained loyal to their masters throughout.

In all, nearly 190,000 Negroes served voluntarily in the Union armies, and their total losses numbered more than 68,000—most of which, like the losses of their white comrades, resulted from disease. They suffered unjust discriminations in both pay and duty assignments and risked the constant threat of death or return to slavery if captured. They endured cruel prejudices from white fellow soldiers, but often these disappeared in the heat of battle. After a fierce battle at Dalton, Georgia, in August, 1864, a white regiment swung their hats and gave three rousing cheers for Colonel Thomas Morgan's crack Negro troops.

After the Civil War the rights of full citizenship would come hard for Negroes everywhere, but in the North they at least had the impetus from their voluntary service in the cause which had brought their freedom. Without this effort, the road would have been even more difficult than it was.

XIV

The Road Ahead

And may-be we, these days, have, too, our own reward. . . . Though not for us the joy of entering at the last the conquer'd city—not ours the chance ever to see with our own eyes the peerless power and splendid *éclat* of the democratic principle . . . there is yet, to whoever is eligible among us, the prophetic vision, the joy of being toss'd in the brave turmoil of these times . . . with the proud consciousness that amid whatever clouds, seductions, or heart-wearying postponements, we have never deserted, never despair'd, never abandoned the faith.

WALT WHITMAN

Southerners paid in full for commencing the Civil War. Their beloved land was left a wasteland of burned homes and fields, twisted railroads and ruined highways, and wrecked or worn-out tools and machinery. The Southern labor, money, and banking systems were destroyed. An exhausted, impoverished, but still defiant people were left almost uniquely unqualified to deal with the social and emotional problems left by the sudden death of slavery. The war had magnified and intensified the very attitudes which had produced the struggle in the first place. Reconstruction would soon open the wounds of humiliation still wider, and in the end only the helpless Negro would be available for vengeance.

The Northern story, however, was quite different. Although the section lost 100,000 more men than did the South, its material losses were offset by enormous economic progress. To meet the necessities of war, ancient economic truths and wisdom were abandoned, and new as well as some older heresies were embraced, often with spectacular results.

It was only natural that the Republicans, as the legitimate heirs of Hamilton, Clay, and Webster, should seize the present opportunity for a final victory over Thomas Jefferson and Andrew Jackson. The obstructing Southern delegations were gone, and the massive needs of the war demanded action. Secession had rendered the very idea of states' rights anathema, and the war had made the federal government omnipotent.

The cost of the war quickly outstripped every new tax, even though the revenues were increased enormously. The Congress assigned each state a quota to be met by direct taxation, created the first national income tax, established the equivalent of a national sales tax, and pushed the tariff to the highest levels in history. The income tax ranged from 3 per cent on incomes above $800 to an astronomical 10 per cent on those above $10,000. The major burden rested squarely upon ordinary people—where it did not restrict the accumulation and investment of money by ambitious and patriotic businessmen eager to build the sinews of war at a profit. Almost 90 per cent of the wartime revenue came from a thirty-page schedule of internal taxes on almost every consumer necessity. All the taxes produced some $667,000,000, but this was entirely inadequate.

Methods for allowing posterity to pay for its blessings were quickly found, however. The national debt rose from $64,844,-000 in 1860 to $2,677,000,000 by the end of 1865, and like Hamilton's debt of the 1790's it served both takers and holders well. With great skill, Jay Cooke's banking firm marketed the bonds for a handsome commission which made Cooke one of America's richest men.

Praising hard-money principles, but pleading necessity, Thaddeus Stevens pushed through a series of acts which provided a total of $431,500,000 in paper currency unsupported by specie, but redeemable in twenty years. The greenbacks quickly began fluctuating at 60 to 70 cents per dollar in relation to gold. The government bonds could be bought with greenbacks, but the legal tender act required that interest be paid in coin. The advantages to the bondholder were obvious, but the shaky credit of the government required a profitable inducement for getting the bonds sold. The interest rate of 7.3 per cent was substantial but not exorbitant, and the steady inflation of consumer prices meant that some of the profits were more apparent than real. With certain well-known exceptions, the financial capitalists of the Civil War fared less profitably than those in industry.

The new national debt made possible a new national banking system which far exceeded any pleasant dream of Henry Clay or nightmare of Andrew Jackson and Thomas Hart Benton. Banks of $50,000 or more could become national banks by accepting certain regulations and buying at least $30,000 worth of government bonds. These banks could then issue national banknotes up to 90 per cent of the value of their government bonds, although a top limit of $300,000,000 in banknotes was placed on the system. Thus the new national banks could collect interest in coin on bonds bought with greenbacks and further interest on the bond-supported paper money loaned to their borrowers. Unfortunately, the bulk of the allowable $300,000,000 quickly became concentrated in the Northeast. A later generation of western radicals would make this injustice one of the bases of American Populism, but as a wartime expedient the overall system performed admirably.

Indeed, just as Hamilton's original program had served America well despite its favoritism toward certain individuals and groups, the financial measures of the Civil War enabled the North to field the best-cared-for army the world had ever seen. The greenbacks, the new banknotes, and the skyrocketing national debt which left a stream of liquid credit and capital in its wake enabled the North to mobilize effectively its superior resources, absorb the fearful economic burden of the war, and enjoy a great burst of economic expansion. During the first year of the war the West suffered from depression and tight credit, and the industrial laboring population was hurt badly by the inflation of prices, but the overall increase of American wealth was spectacular. Northerners loaned their government some $2,600,000,000 worth of man-hours, resources, skills, and material, and the greenbacks and banknotes were a vital part of the productive process.

Other Whiggish triumphs quickly followed. The Homestead Act, the Morrill Land Grant Act, the Contract Labor Law for immigrants, and the huge grants of loans and land by which the transcontinental railroads were built through a vast unoccupied territory were all quickly enacted.

The government of the United States had become a paternalistic engine of progress, and the practice if not the doctrine of laissez-faire was gone forever. For another generation the newly assumed powers of the government would be manipulated by the fastest grabbers, and America's great resources would be subjected to what Vernon L. Parrington later called The Great Barbecue. Much injustice and exploitation would be part of the price paid by America for its new national wealth and power. Ultimately, however, the process of democracy would throw control of the nation back into the hands of those ready to use its powers for regulation, adjustment, balance and justice.

In 1865, thoughtful Americans could look back on the years since 1837 with mingled sorrow, relief, and pride.

An empire had been seized from Mexico, and a clear title to a proper share of the vast Oregon country had been gained. The young nation now stretched across the continent from ocean to ocean. True, the despoiling of Mexico had tarnished somewhat the image of innocent purity most Americans enjoyed assigning to their country, but the concept of manifest destiny was an effective healing unguent for sore consciences.

Manifest destiny, however, had provided new territories for competition between slave and non-slave states, while its arguments themselves were an implied rebuke to slavery. When the racism and defensive aggressiveness of slavery were blended with democratic idealism, nationalism, and successful imperialism, the South's peculiar institution had become indefensible.

The price was high but in the end the cancer of slavery was gone, the Union had been preserved, the national sense of mission had been renewed, and the ancient dream of an America dedicated to freedom, justice, and equality of opportunity

remained. Convalescence would be long and hard, but the
patient would recover.

The racism left in the wake of slavery was still a crippling
disease, and the temptations of the new opportunities for economic power would become a serious barrier to the achievement
of the American dream. An age of corruption, greed, and
exploitation lay directly ahead. Still, a purer and stronger
America faced the future in 1865, and its more idealistic citizens
did not doubt that however long and difficult the road ahead
might be, their descendants would finally overcome, and the
bright potential of American life would some day be a reality.

Important Dates

1619   First slaves landed in Jamestown, Virginia

1832–33   Nullification controversy

1835   Various Southern states pass laws against abolitionists and abolition literature, and demand federal legislation to bar such literature from the mails

1836   Legislation to permit postmasters to intercept publications barred by the legislature of a particular state defeated in the Senate

Emergence of the Loco Foco faction to power in the New York Democratic party

Texas wins independence from Mexico. Congress passes resolutions for recognition of Texas after bitter debate

1837   President Jackson recognizes Texas but rejects offer of annexation

Van Buren becomes President

Economic panic and depression

Fierce congressional debate over the petitions for abolition of slavery in the District of Columbia. Adoption of gag rule

Murder of the abolitionist editor Elijah P. Lovejoy at Alton, Illinois

Important Dates

The Death of Slavery

Death of President Taylor. Fillmore becomes President

North angry over fugitive slave law

1851–60 Constant agitation in both North and South over fugitive slave problem and various rescues and recaptures

1852 *Uncle Tom's Cabin* published

Franklin Pierce elected President

1853 Gadsden Purchase

1854 Kansas-Nebraska act and "Appeal of the Independent Democrats"

Establishment of the New England Emigrant Aid Society

Founding of the Republican party

Founding of the Know-Nothing party

The Ostend manifesto

1855 Elections in Kansas and "Bleeding Kansas"

1856 Civil war in Kansas. John Brown murders five colonists

The Kansas issue in Congress. The caning of Charles Sumner

Nomination of Frémont as sectional candidate by Republicans and nomination of ex-President Fillmore by the Know-Nothings

Election of President James Buchanan

1857 Dred Scott decision

Debate over the Lecompton constitution for Kansas

Brief economic panic and depression

Publication of *The Impending Crisis of the South* by Hinton Rowan Helper

1858 Congress sends Lecompton constitution back to Kansas for another popular vote and it is defeated

Lincoln "house divided" speech

Lincoln-Douglas debates

Seward "irrepressible conflict" speech

Republican success in Northern congressional and state elections

1859 John Brown's raid

New efforts made to revive the African slave trade

1860 Davis resolutions for a territorial slave code

Lincoln's Cooper Union speech

Breakup of the Democratic party at the Charleston convention

Nomination and election of Lincoln over Douglas, Bell, and Breckinridge

1861 Secession of the Southern states and formation of the Confederacy

Important Dates

Unsuccessful compromise efforts in Congress
Lincoln's first inaugural
Firing on Fort Sumter
First battle of Bull Run
McClellan placed in command
Trent affair
Establishment of Congressional Joint Committee on the Conduct of the War

1862   Union wins successful battles at Mill Springs, Kentucky; Fort Donelson and Shiloh, Tennessee
Occupation of New Orleans
Monitor vs. *Merrimac*
McClellan advance on Richmond and Jackson's Valley campaign
Robert E. Lee given command of the Army of Northern Virginia
After Seven Days' Battle Union advance on Richmond stopped
Defeat of General Pope at second Bull Run
Lee's invasion of Maryland and defeat at Antietam
Defeat of General Burnside at Fredericksburg

1863   Emancipation Proclamation takes effect on January 1
First conscription act. Draft riots
Establishment of national banking system
Homestead act
Confederate raiders *Alabama* and *Florida* escape from England to sea, wreak havoc on Union shipping
Defeat of General Hooker at Chancellorsville
Siege and capture of Vicksburg
Battle of Gettysburg
Battles of Chickamauga and Chattanooga

1864   Grant takes command of Union forces
Battles of the Wilderness, Spotsylvania, Cold Harbor, Petersburg
Sherman's march through Georgia and Sheridan's march through Virginia
Reelection of Lincoln

1865   Lincoln's second inaugural
Surrender at Appomattox

Suggested Reading

The literature of this period is so voluminous that any compilation is certain to omit many valuable books.

An excellent starting point is Thomas J. Pressly, *Americans Interpret Their Civil War* (1962), and the briefer and older work by Howard K. Beale, "What Historians Have Said About the Causes of the Civil War" (Social Science Research Council Bulletin 54: "Theory and Practice in Historical Study" [1946]). These books summarize various interpretations period by period and author by author. A broad knowledge of bibliography can also be gained by reading the sample selections from various authors in the pertinent pamphlet volumes of the "Problems of American Civilization Series" developed by the Department of American Studies at Amherst College. These include *The Causes of the American Civil War, Slavery as a Cause of the Civil War, Lincoln and the Coming of the Civil War,* and *The Compromise of 1850.* Two brief articles, Charles W. Ramsdell, "The Changing Interpretations of the Civil War," *The Journal of Southern History,* Vol. 3 (1937), and David Donald, "American Historians and the Causes of the Civil War," *The South Atlantic Quarterly,* Vol. 59 (1960), make similar contributions.

Suggested Reading

Probably the best of the early "Southern conspiracy and Northern crusade" versions are those of Joshua R. Giddings, *History of the Rebellion: Its Authors and Causes*; Horace Greeley, *The American Conflict* (2 vols., 1864–66); Henry Wilson, *History of the Rise and Fall of the Slave Power in America* (3 vols., 1872–77); and the *Life and Times of Frederick Douglass Written by Himself* (1881). Douglass, a former slave, argued also that if the South had accepted the Northern concessions, slavery might have continued indefinitely. The most scholarly expressions of this view were those of the German professor Hermann Eduard Von Holst, *The Constitutional and Political History of the United States* (8 vols., 1876–92); and James Schouler, *History of the United States of America under the Constitution* (5 vols., 1880–91). Schouler, however, did argue that the Southern people supported the secession movement.

The classic expressions of the Southern constitutional view are Jefferson Davis, *The Rise and Fall of the Confederate Government* (2 vols., 1881); Alexander H. Stephens, *A Constitutional View of the Late War between the States* (2 vols., 1868–70); and Albert T. Bledsoe, *The War between the States* (1915).

Perhaps the pioneer of the deterministic interpreters was John W. Draper, *History of the American Civil War* (3 vols., 1867–70), who blamed the war primarily on differences in climate. Draper, however, while excusing Southerners' actions, charged the Southern Slave Power with full responsibility.

Deterministic theories of history swept through the world in the late nineteenth century, and when adapted to the Civil War they did much to hasten the process of reconciliation. The concept of an inevitable war, unavoidable by either side, removed the burdens of guilt.

While Schouler in the work cited above and John Burgess, *The Middle Period 1817–1858* (1897), shared the traditional view of the war as a crusade against slavery, they at least implied that the Southerners were victims of circumstances rather than villains. James Ford Rhodes, *History of the United States from the Compromise of 1850* (7 vols., 1893–1906), equally convinced that slavery and its evils had caused the war, saw the institution as a Southern burden rather than a sin, and blamed the technology of cotton-raising. Woodrow Wilson, *Division and Reunion 1829–1889* (1893) blamed the processes of growth and evolution. Although he did not deal

The Death of Slavery

directly with the war problem, Frederick Jackson Turner also contributed much to the idea of American history and development as a cosmic process. His essay collections, *The Frontier in American History* (1920) and *The Significance of Sections in American History* (1932) and his book *The United States, 1830–1850* (1935) contribute much to an understanding of the period. Edward Channing, *A History of the United States* (6 vols., 1905–25); and John B. McMaster, *A History of the People of the United States from the Revolution to the Civil War* (9 vols., 1883–1913), likewise saw an irrepressible conflict between differing social, political, economic, and philosophical systems created essentially by circumstances. In a later work, Arthur C. Cole, *The Irrepressible Conflict 1850–1865* (1934), combines most of these viewpoints.

Naturally enough, pro-Southern historians in the same period began to reject the older constitutional arguments and defend the Southern society as one of many virtues which did the best it could with its faults and problems. Among these were William E. Dodd, *The Cotton Kingdom* (1918), *Statesmen of the Old South* (1911), and *Expansion and Conflict* (1918); Ulrich B. Phillips, *American Negro Slavery* (1918), and *Life and Labor in the Old South* (1929). Far more vindictive against the North were Frank L. Owsley, "The Irrepressible Conflict," in Twelve Southerners, *I'll Take My Stand* (1930), and "The Fundamental Cause of the Civil War: Egocentric Sectionalism," *The Journal of Southern History*, Vol. 7 (1941); and Charles Ramsdell, "Lincoln and Fort Sumter," *The Journal of Southern History*, Vol. 3 (1937), and "The Natural Limits of Slavery Expansion," *The Mississippi Valley Historical Review*, Vol. 16 (1929). Ramsdell argued that Lincoln deliberately provoked the South into firing on Fort Sumter. Owsley accused the North of seeking to force its industrial civilization upon the South.

The Beardian thesis of economic determinism may be found in various articles and books. The appropriate chapters in Volume II of Charles A. and Mary R. Beard, *The Rise of American Civilization* (2 vols., 1927), state the case clearly. Vernon L. Parrington's beautifully written *Main Currents in American Thought* (3 vols., 1927–30), in Volume II echoes Beard and provides many provocative essays on the thinkers and opinion-makers of the era.

Often described as the earliest "revisionist" is Mary Scrugham, *The Peaceable Americans of 1860–1861: A Study in Public Opinion*

Suggested Reading

(1921). The basic thesis, however, goes back at least as far as Thomas Hart Benton's *Thirty Years View* (2 vols., 1854–56), in which the senator blamed the growing conflict and likely future war on extremism, distortion, exaggeration, and partisan politics. Benton's bitter enemy, Senator Henry S. Foote, *War of the Rebellion* (1886), reached the same conclusions and like Benton placed most of the blame upon his own section. Samuel S. Cox, *Eight Years in Congress* (1865), took much the same view. Revisionism also included a new approach to abolitionism, illustrated by Gilbert H. Barnes, *The Antislavery Impulse, 1830–1844* (1933). The best known of the modern revisionists are James G. Randall and Avery O. Craven. The Randall view is clearly stated in "The Blundering Generation," *The Mississippi Valley Historical Review*, Vol. 27 (1940), and in *Civil War and Reconstruction* (1937). The latter book was revised somewhat in a new edition brought out by David Donald in 1961. Craven's *The Repressible Conflict, 1830–1861* (1939), and *Coming of the Civil War* (1942; rev. ed. 1957) are beautifully written expositions. Although he reached retirement age in 1951, Craven has remained a vigorous scholar and teacher who continues to develop new ideas. Among his later works, some of which have modified several of his earlier concepts, are *The Growth of Southern Nationalism, 1848–1861* (1953), *Civil War in the Making* (1959), numerous articles, and a collection of writings titled *An Historian and the Civil War* (1964). From *The Repressible Conflict* Craven has swung back to a view of peoples struggling in the grip of impersonal forces such as the Industrial Revolution, modern technology and communications, growing interdependence, and social problems not of their own making.

The earlier starting point of Randall and Craven has been shared by George Fort Milton, *The Eve of Conflict: Stephen A. Douglas and the Needless War* (1934), Roy F. Nichols, *The Disruption of American Democracy* (1949), and Allan Nevins, *Ordeal of the Union* (4 vols., 1947–50). Milton offers a somewhat shrill defense of Douglas and moderation against the wickedness of selfish politicians and extremists. Nichols' work is a more scholarly treatise on the disrupting effects of partisan politics. Nevins' massive, thorough, and excitingly written study is somewhat inconsistent, as he poses the fundamental problems and deep-seated sectional differences involved and then appears to blame the leaders of the day

The Death of Slavery

for not overcoming them. Kenneth M. Stampp, *And the War Came: The North and the Secession Crisis 1880–1861* (1950), blames the secession upon irreconcilable differences, but questions the necessity for war and wonders just why the North would not permit the South to secede in peace. Implicit in this view is a feeling that the war was not worth its cost. The earlier work by David Potter, *Lincoln and His Party in Secession Crisis* (1942), stressed the failure of Lincoln to work for compromise before hostilities began. Richard N. Current, *Lincoln and the First Shot* (1963) offers still another look at this moment and corrects some earlier myths. David Donald's brilliant study *Charles Sumner and the Coming of the Civil War* (1960) also starts essentially from a revisionist viewpoint.

The final crisis is also discussed brilliantly in two essay compilations, *Politics and the Crisis of 1860* (1961), edited by Norman A. Graebner, and *The Crisis of the Union 1860–1861* (1965), edited by George H. Knoles. Two important books revising earlier versions of the Kansas struggles are James C. Malin, *John Brown and the Legend of Fifty-six* (1942) and the *Nebraska Question* (1953). Two excellent collections on *Southern Editorials on Secession* (1931), edited by Dwight L. Dumond, and *Northern Editorials on Secession* (2 vols., 1942), edited by H. C. Perkins.

Books which do not specialize in the war problem, but which shed much light on American character and thought during the period include Carl R. Fish, *The Rise of the Common Man, 1830–1850* (1927); Daniel J. Boorstin, *The Americans: The Colonial Experience* (1959), and *The Americans: The National Experience* (1965); Charles and Mary Beard, *The American Spirit* (1942); Vernon L. Parrington, *Main Currents in American Thought* (3 vols., 1927–30); Merle Curti, *The Growth of American Thought* (1951); Ralph N. Gabriel, *The Course of American Democratic Thought* (2d ed. 1956); Richard Hofstadter, *The American Political Tradition and the Men Who Made It* (1948); Arthur M. Schlesinger, *The American as Reformer* (1950); and Arthur M. Schlesinger, Jr., *The Age of Jackson* (1945). Alexis de Tocqueville, *Democracy in America* (4 vols., 1835–40), should be sampled by every student.

The antislavery movement is chronicled from different vantage points by Albert B. Hart, *Slavery and Abolition, 1831–1841* (1906); Russell B. Nye, *William Lloyd Garrison and the Humanitarian Re-*

Suggested Reading

formers (1955); Gilbert H. Barnes, *The Anti-Slavery Impulse, 1833–1844* (1933); Louis Filler, *The Crusade against Slavery, 1830–1860* (1960); Dwight L. Dumond, *Antislavery: The Crusade for Freedom in America* (1961); Larry Gara, *The Liberty Line: The Legend of the Underground Railroad* (1961); Henry S. Commager, *Theodore Parker* (1936); Betty Fladeland, *James Gillespie Birney: Slaveholder to Abolitionist* (1955); and I. H. Bartlett, *Wendell Phillips: Brahmin Rebel* (1961).

Good accounts of the proslavery story are W. S. Jenkins, *Pro-Slavery Thought in the Old South* (1935); and Harvey Wish, *George Fitzhugh: Propagandist of the Old South* (1943). Wish has also edited an invaluable collection of contemporary accounts of slavery, both pro and con, *Slavery in the South* (1964). Fitzhugh's books, *Sociology for the South* (1954), and *Cannibals All: or, Slaves Without Masters* (1857), remain the classic Southern defense.

Ulrich B. Phillips, *American Negro Slavery* (1918) and *Life and Labor in the Old South* (1929), emphasize the paternalism and milder aspects of slavery. Kenneth M. Stampp, *The Peculiar Institution* (1956), stresses both the evils and the profitability of slavery. Disagreeing with those who have argued that slavery was ultimately doomed for economic reasons, Stampp as well as Alfred H. Conrad and John R. Meyer, "The Economics of Slavery in the Ante-Bellum South," *The Journal of Political Economy*, Vol. 66 (1958), insist that slavery was highly profitable and therefore destined to a long future had the war not come. Stanley M. Elkins, *Slavery: A Problem in American Institutional and Intellectual Life* (1959), deals brilliantly with the psychological impact of slavery on American life. What slavery meant to the slave himself is more vividly revealed in the *Life and Times of Frederick Douglass Written by Himself* (1881); Booker T. Washington, *Up From Slavery* (1940 [paper]); George W. Williams, *History of the Negro Race in America from 1619 to 1880* (2 vols., 1883); and John Hope Franklin, *From Slavery to Freedom* (1947). A highly significant but rarely discussed form of slavery is described by Richard C. Wade, *Slavery in the Cities: The South, 1820–1860* (1964).

The plight of the Negro generally is well described by Leon F. Litwack, *North of Slavery: The Negro in the Free States* (1961); and William Stanton, *The Leopard's Spots: Scientific Attitudes toward Race in America, 1815–59* (1960).

The Death of Slavery

Valuable studies of the unique features and developments in the sections include Perry Miller, *The New England Mind* (1956); Van Wyck Brooks, *The Flowering of New England, 1815–1865* (1936); Alice F. Tyler, *Freedom's Ferment: Phases of American Social History to 1860* (1944); Norman Ware, *The Early New England Cotton Manufacture: The Industrial Worker 1840–1860* (1924), and *Study in Industrial Beginnings* (1931); J. G. Rayback, *History of American Labor* (1959); Marcus Hansen, *The Immigrant in American History* (1940); Oscar Handlin, *The Uprooted* (1951); Thomas C. Cochrane and William Miller, *The Age of Enterprise: Social History of Industrial America* (1942); John R. Commons, *History of Labour in the United States* (4 vols., 1918–35); Samuel Eliot Morison, *Maritime History of Massachusetts, 1783–1860* (1921); O. B. Frothingham, *Transcendentalism in New England* (1876); Russell B. Nye, *Fettered Freedom: Civil Liberties and the Slavery Controversy, 1830–1860* (1949); Paul Monroe, *The Founding of the American Public School System* (1940); Lewis Mumford, *The Golden Day* (1926); R. S. Fletcher, *A History of Oberlin College from Its Foundation through the Civil War* (2 vols., 1943); William H. Siebert, *The Underground Railroad from Slavery to Freedom* (1898); H. C. Hubbart, *The Older Middle West, 1840–1680* (1936); Paul W. Gates, *The Farmer's Age, 1815–1860* (1960); Ray Billington, *Westward Expansion* (1949); and *The Protestant Crusade, 1800–1860* (1938); Frederic L. Paxson, *History of the American Frontier, 1763–1893* (1924); Ralph H. Gabriel, *The Lure of the Frontier* (1929); J. W. Oliver, *History of American Technology* (1956); G. R. Taylor, *The Transportation Revolution* (1951); A. H. Sanford, *The Story of Agriculture in the United States* (1916); the previously cited works by Turner; Frederick L. Olmsted, *The Cotton Kingdom* (1861; new ed. 1953); W. J. Cash, *The Mind of the South* (1941); Clement Eaton, *A History of the Old South* (1949), *The Growth of Southern Civilization, 1790–1860* (1961); and *Freedom of Thought in the Old South* (1940); William B. Hesseltine and D. L. Smiley, *The South in American History* (1960); R. S. Cotterill, *The Old South* (1939); Frank L. Owsley, *Plain Folk of the Old South* (1949); E. Q. Hawk, *Economic History of the South* (1934); W. R. Taylor, *Cavalier and Yankee: The Old South and American National Character* (1961); Charles S. Sydnor, *The De-*

Suggested Reading

velopment of Southern Sectionalism, 1819–1848 (1948); Craven, Growth of Southern Nationalism (1953); and John Hope Franklin, The Militant South (1956).

The story of Texas and the Mexican War has generated much fascinating history. Albert K. Weinberg, Manifest Destiny (1935), and Frederick Merk, Manifest Destiny and Mission in American History (1963), disagree on the nature and the impact of the expansionist spirit. See also Bernard DeVoto, The Year of Decision, 1846 (1943); Dodd, Expansion and Conflict (1915); Norman A. Graebner, Empire on the Pacific (1955); William C. Binkley, The Texas Revolution (1952); Jesse S. Reeves, American Diplomacy under Tyler and Polk (1907); George L. Rives, The United States and Mexico, 1821–1848 (2 vols., 1913); E. C. Barker, Mexico and Texas, 1821–1835 (1928); Justin H. Smith, The War with Mexico (2 vols., 1919); R. S. Henry, Story of the Mexican War (1950); O. A. Singletary, The Mexican War (1960); and several biographies.

Expansion into Oregon is beautifully described by Francis Parkman, The Oregon Trail (1849 and many later editions). See also O. O. Winther, The Great Northwest (1947); M. C. Jacobs, Winning Oregon (1938); and Charles H. Carey, A General History of Oregon (1935).

Probably the most readable of the military histories of the Civil War are those of Bruce Catton, Mr. Lincoln's Army (1951), Glory Road (1952), A Stillness at Appomattox (1954), This Hallowed Ground (1956), and Grant Moves South (1960). The previously cited Civil War and Reconstruction (1961) by James G. Randall and David Donald remains one of the best accounts of the war as a whole. T. Harry Williams, Lincoln and the Radicals (1941), treats the Congressional Committee on the Conduct of the War with justifiable harshness. Williams, Lincoln and His Generals (1952), is also excellent. The Southern counterpart of Catton is Douglas S. Freeman, Lee's Lieutenants (3 vols., 1942–44). K. P. Williams, Lincoln Finds a General (5 vols., 1949–59), is a massive source of information. A listing of everything of merit written about the Civil War would require another volume, and the following list is admittedly only fragmentary: The Blue and the Gray (2 vols., 1950), edited by Henry S. Commager; Divided We Fought (1953) and Why the North Won the Civil War (1960), both edited by

The Death of Slavery

David Donald; J. B. Mitchell, *Decisive Battles of the Civil War* (1955); Ned Bradford, *Battles and Leaders of the Civil War* (1956); *The Civil War: The American Iliad* (2 vols., 1956), edited by Otto Eisenschiml, Ralph Newman, and E. B. Long; Glenn Tucker, *High Tide at Gettysburg* (1958) and *Chickamauga* (1961); Edward Steere, *The Wilderness Campaign* (1960); Clifford Dowdey, *Lee's Last Campaign* (1960); Fred A. Shannon, *The Organization and Administration of the Union Army, 1861–1865* (2 vols., 1928); B. I. Wiley, *The Life of Johnny Reb, the Common Soldier of the Confederacy* (1943) and *The Life of Billy Yank, the Common Soldier of the Union* (1952); J. K. Barnes, *The Medical and Surgical History of the War of the Rebellion* (6 vols., 1870–88); Stanley Horn, *The Army of Tennessee* (1941); and J. C. Ropes and W. R. Livermore, *The Story of the Civil War* (4 vols., 1894–1913). The role of Negroes in the war is described in George W. Williams, *History of Negro Troops in the War of the Rebellion* (1888), and an able modern study by Dudley T. Cornish, *The Sable Arm* (1956).

The naval history of the Civil War has been chronicled in several excellent books, which include V. C. Jones, *The Civil War at Sea* (3 vols., 1960–62); R. S. West, *Mr. Lincoln's Navy* (1957); J. M. Merrill, *The Rebel Shore* (1957); Bern Anderson, *By Sea and by River* (1962); and W. M. Robinson, Jr., *The Confederate Privateers* (1928).

Political, economic, and social problems of the war have been well described by Randall, *The Confiscation of Property during the Civil War* (1913) and *Constitutional Problems under Lincoln* (1926); William B. Hesseltine, *Civil War Prisons: A Study in War Psychology* (1930); E. M. Lonn, *Desertion during the Civil War* (1928); R. S. Henry, *The Story of the Confederacy* (1957); E. Merton Coulter, *The Confederate States of America* (1950); Frank L. Owsley, *State Rights in the Confederacy* (1925) and *Behind the Lines in the Southern Confederacy* (1944); D. R. Dewey, *Financial History of the United States* (12th ed., 1936); Zechariah Chaffee, Jr., *Freedom of Speech* (1910); George F. Milton, *Abraham Lincoln and the Fifth Column* (1942); Wood Gray, *The Hidden Civil War: The Story of the Copperheads* (1941); Emerson D. Fite, *Social and Industrial Conditions in the North during the Civil War* (1910); Mary B. Chesnut, *A Diary from Dixie* (1905); Francis B. Simkins and J. W. Patton, *Women of the Confederacy* (1936); B. I. Wiley,

Suggested Reading

Southern Negroes, 1861–1865 (1938) and *The Plain People of the South* (1943); H. H. Cunningham, *Doctors in Gray* (1958); George W. Adams, *Doctors in Blue: The Medical History of the Union Army* (1952); Margaret Leech, *Reveille in Washington* (1941); and Bernard Weisberger, *Reporters for the Union* (1943).

The relations of the belligerents with Europe are described by E. D. Adams, *Great Britain and the American Civil War* (2 vols., 1925 and 1957); Donaldson Jordan and E. J. Pratt, *Europe and the American Civil War* (1931); Frank L. Owsley, *King Cotton Diplomacy* (1931 and 1959); Frederic Bancroft, *The Life of William H. Seward* (2 vols., 1900); Margaret Clapp, *Forgotten First Citizen: John Bigelow* (1947); and M. B. Duberman, *Charles Francis Adams, 1807–1889* (1961).

The biographies of this period offer many fascinating details and perceptive interpretations. The enormous Lincoln bibliography is graced by such works as Benjamin P. Thomas, *Abraham Lincoln* (1952); Reinhard H. Luthin, *The Real Abraham Lincoln* (1960); James G. Randall, *Lincoln the President* (4 vols., 1945–55), with Richard N. Current as co-author of Volume IV; Current, *Mr. Lincoln* (1957) and *The Lincoln Nobody Knows* (1958); Carl Sandburg, *Abraham Lincoln: The War Years* (4 vols., 1949), and *Abraham Lincoln* (1954); David Donald, *Lincoln Reconsidered: Essays on the Civil War Era* (1956); Albert Beveridge, *Abraham Lincoln 1809–1858* (2 vols., 1928); and J. G. Nicolay and John Hay, *Abraham Lincoln: A History* (10 vols., 1890; abridged ed. 1966). Nicolay and Hay were Lincoln's secretaries and offer many firsthand accounts of controversial events. Roy P. Basler, *The Collected Works of Abraham Lincoln* (9 vols., 1953), is a basic original source. Specialized Lincoln studies and monographs include Burton J. Hendrick, *Lincoln's War Cabinet* (1946); William B. Hesseltine, *Lincoln and the War Governors* (1948); Harry J. Carman and Reinhard J. Luthin, *Lincoln and the Patronage* (1943); T. Harry Williams, *Lincoln and the Radicals* (1941); R. S. Harper, *Lincoln and the Press* (1951); R. V. Bruce, *Lincoln and the Tools of War* (1956); C. R. Ballard, *The Military Genius of Abraham Lincoln* (1952); a brilliant reappraisal by Don E. Fehrenbacher, *Prelude to Greatness: Lincoln in the 1850's* (1962); and William E. Barringer, *Lincoln's Rise to Power* (1937), and *A House Dividing* (1945).

Calhoun receives friendly and favorable treatment from Charles

The Death of Slavery

M. Wiltse, *John C. Calhoun, Nullifier, 1829–1839* (1949), and *John C. Calhoun, Sectionalist, 1840–1850* (1951); and Margaret L. Coit, *John C. Calhoun: American Portrait* (1950). More critical and more realistic are Richard N. Current, *John C. Calhoun* (1963); G. M. Capers, *John C. Calhoun—Opportunist: A Reappraisal* (1960); and Richard Hofstadter in the Calhoun chapter of *The American Political Tradition and the Men Who Made It* (1948).

Thomas Hart Benton, the bitter enemy of Calhoun, has been recently portrayed by E. B. Smith, *Magnificent Missourian: The Life of Thomas Hart Benton* (1958), and William N. Chambers, *Old Bullion Benton, Senator from the New West* (1956).

Henry Clay, the great peacemaker, is perhaps best described by Carl Schurz, *Henry Clay* (2 vols., 1899); Glyndon G. Van Deusen, *Life of Henry Clay* (1937); and Clement Eaton, *Henry Clay and the Art of American Politics* (1957). The latter work captures the real essence of Clay's contribution.

Daniel Webster receives his due from Charles M. Fuess, *Daniel Webster* (2 vols., 1930), and Richard N. Current, *Daniel Webster and the Rise of National Conservatism* (1955). A highly readable popular study which leans heavily upon biographical analysis is Gerald W. Johnson, *America's Silver Age: The Statecraft of Clay, Webster, and Calhoun* (1939).

The latest study of Douglas is G. M. Capers, *Stephen A. Douglas, Defender of the Union* (1959), and others are in progress. The older book by Allen Johnson, *Stephen A. Douglas* (1908), and the previously cited George F. Milton, *The Eve of Conflict: Stephen A. Douglas and the Needless War* (1934), are adequate. See also *Created Equal? The Complete Lincoln-Douglas Debates of 1858* (1958), edited by Paul M. Angle; and H. V. Jaffa, *Crisis of the House Divided: An Interpretation of the Issues in the Lincoln-Douglas Debates* (1959).

Other valuable studies of Northern leaders include David Donald, *Charles Sumner and the Coming of the Civil War* (1960); Ralph V. Harlow, *Gerrit Smith, Philanthropist and Reformer* (1939); R. L. Rusk, *The Life of Ralph Waldo Emerson* (1949); Allan Nevins, *Frémont, Pathmarker of the West* (1955); F. B. Woodford, *Lewis Cass* (1950); Robert J. Rayback, *Millard Fillmore* (1959); Glyndon G. Van Deusen, *Thurlow Weed* (1947) and *Horace Greeley* (1953); W. H. Hale, *Horace Greeley, Voice of the People* (1950); Frederic

Suggested Reading

Bancroft, *William H. Seward* (2 vols., 1900); Roy F. Nichols, *Franklin Pierce, Young Hickory of the Granite Plains* (1931); O. G. Villard, *John Brown, 1800–1859: A Biography Fifty Years After* (1910); R. P. Warren, *John Brown: The Making of a Martyr* (1929); James C. Malin, *John Brown and the Legend of Fifty-six* (1942); P. S. Klein, *President James Buchanan* (1962); Hans L. Trefousse, *Benjamin Franklin Wade* (1963); Richard N. Current, *Old Thad Stevens* (1942); Benjamin P. Thomas and H. M. Hyman, *Stanton* (1962); Thomas G. and Marva R. Belden, *So Fell the Angels* (1956), a study of Salmon P. Chase; Don E. Fehrenbacher, *Chicago Giant, a Biography of "Long John" Wentworth* (1957); and Holman Hamilton, *Zachary Taylor, Soldier in the White House* (1951). While he was originally a Southerner, Taylor must be considered a pro-Northern President.

Colorful but scholarly biographies of Southern leaders include Burton J. Hendrick, *Statesmen of the Lost Cause* (1939); Gamaliel Bradford, *Confederate Portraits* (1914); William E. Dodd, *Jefferson Davis* (1907); Hudson Strode, *Jefferson Davis: American Patriot* (1955); H. J. Eckenrode, *Jefferson Davis, President of the South* (1923); Avery O. Craven, *Edmund Ruffin, Southerner* (1932); Broadus Mitchell, *William Gregg* (1928); Laura A. White, *Robert Barnwell Rhett: Father of Secession* (1931); Ulrich B. Phillips, *Robert Toombs* (1913); O. C. Skipper, *J. D. B. DeBow: Magazinist of the Old South* (1958); D. L. Smiley, *Lion of White Hall: The Life of Cassius M. Clay* (1962); Louis Pendleton, *Alexander H. Stephens* (1908); Rudolph von Abele, *Alexander H. Stephens* (1946); R. D. Meade, *Judah P. Benjamin* (1943); W. E. Parrish, *David Rice Atchison* (1961); and Oliver P. Chitwood, *John Tyler* (1939).

James K. Polk has been perceptively studied by Charles G. Sellers, *James K. Polk, Jacksonian* (1957) and *James K. Polk, Continentalist* (1966), and by Ernest I. McCormac, *James K. Polk* (1922). See also the two published editions of Polk's diary of his presidential years by Milo M. Quaife (4 vols., 1910) and Allan Nevins (1929). Marquis James, *The Raven* (1929), is an exciting account of Sam Houston. Joseph H. Parks, *John Bell of Tennessee* (1950), describes still another Southern moderate.

Among the better military biographies are C. W. Elliot, *Winfield Scott* (1937); Holman Hamilton, *Zachary Taylor, Soldier of the Republic* (1946); Douglas S. Freeman, *R. E. Lee* (4 vols., 1934–35);

The Death of Slavery

Burke Davis, *Gray Fox* (1956); Frank Vandiver, *Mighty Stonewall* (1957); T. Harry Williams, *Beauregard, Napoleon in Gray* (1955); R. S. Henry, *"First with the Most" Forrest* (1944); J. W. Thomason, Jr., *Jeb Stuart* (1930); J. P. Dyer, *The Gallant Hood* (1950); J. F. C. Fuller, *The Generalship of Ulysses S. Grant* (1929); Bruce Catton, *Grant Moves South* (1960); Freeman Cleaves, *The Rock of Chickamauga* (1948)—a study of G. H. Thomas; W. S. Myers, *A Study in Personality, General George Brinton McClellan* (1934); H. J. Eckenrode and Bryan Conrad, *George B. McClellan* (1941); W. W. Hassler, Jr., *General George B. McClellan* (1957); Lloyd Lewis, *Sherman, Fighting Prophet* (1932); Richard O'Connor, *Sheridan the Inevitable* (1953); T. Harry Williams, *McClellan, Sherman and Grant* (1962); W. A. Roberts, *Semmes of the Alabama* (1938); and C. L. Lewis, *David Glasgow Farragut* (2 vols., 1941–43). A biography of Admiral Samuel Phillips Lee is needed.

To all of the many authors whose able and valuable works are omitted from the foregoing list I humbly apologize.

Acknowledgments

I am grateful to many who have helped me write this book.

To the librarians and curators who make the writing of history possible.

To Avery Craven, William T. Hutchinson, Walter Johnson, Verton Queener, Jessie Heron, and Effie C. Huffaker, for their teaching.

To the many authors from whom I have gained information and insight.

To the Social Science Research Council for financial assistance on a related subject which added to my knowledge of this one.

To Michael Collins who suggested the radio lectures which became the first draft of this book, and to station WOI, Ames, Iowa, for broadcasting them.

To Colonel E. Brooke Lee for hospitality and information.

To Betty Jean McCormick and Susan Palmer for typing, to Kathleen Hall for proofreading, and to Carole Kennedy for cheerful assistance.

To Clarence H. Matterson for kindness and patience.

To my fellow politicians who make those of the nineteenth century easier to understand.

To my wife, Jean, for unselfishness, assistance, encouragement, and inspiration.

217

Index

Index

Index

Index

THE CHICAGO HISTORY OF AMERICAN CIVILIZATION

Daniel J. Boorstin, Editor

Edmund S. Morgan, *The Birth of the Republic: 1763–89*
Marcus Cunliffe, *The Nation Takes Shape: 1789–1837*
Elbert B. Smith, *The Death of Slavery: The United States, 1837–65*
John Hope Franklin, *Reconstruction: After the Civil War*
Samuel P. Hays, *The Response to Industrialism: 1885–1914*
William E. Leuchtenburg, *The Perils of Prosperity: 1914–32*
Dexter Perkins, *The New Age of Franklin Roosevelt: 1932–45*
Herbert Agar, *The Price of Power: America since 1945*

Robert H. Bremner, *American Philanthropy*
Harry L. Coles, *The War of 1812*
Carl W. Condit, *American Building: Materials and Techniques from the Beginning of the Colonial Settlements to the Present*
Richard M. Dorson, *American Folklore*
John Tracy Ellis, *American Catholicism*
Nathan Glazer, *American Judaism*
William T. Hagan, *American Indians*
Winthrop S. Hudson, *American Protestantism*
Maldwyn Allen Jones, *American Immigration*
Robert G. McCloskey, *The American Supreme Court*
Howard H. Peckham, *The War for Independence: A Military History*
Howard H. Peckham, *The Colonial Wars: 1689–1762*
Henry Pelling, *American Labor*
John B. Rae, *The American Automobile: A Brief History*
Charles P. Roland, *The Confederacy*
Irving L. Sablosky, *American Music*
Otis A. Singletary, *The Mexican War*
John F. Stover, *American Railroads*
Bernard A. Weisberger, *The American Newspaperman*

Most of the books in the series are available in both cloth and paperback editions.

THE UNIVERSITY OF CHICAGO PRESS

Sablosky, Irving L., *American Music*